DYING TO LIVE

A Personal Journey Through Terminal Illness Using Spiritual-Logic

Helen K Emms
Inspiring Spiritual-Logic

lip

First published in 2012 by:

Live It Publishing
27 Old Gloucester Road
London, United Kingdom.
WC1N 3AX
www.liveitpublishing.com

ISBN 978-1-906954-57-4 (pbk)

Dedication

I would like to dedicate this book to the following people:

First and foremost to my dearest mother, for the courage, strength and compassion she demonstrated to us over the last few months of her life. She was a very good role model.

To my partner, Murielle, whose caring, understanding and unwavering support enabled me to give the level of care to my mother that I did.

To my brother and sisters for their personal contributions in supporting Mum's last few months.

Finally, I wish to thank all those who work in any capacity helping people during this part of their journey. They do a wonderfully important job under very challenging conditions. These people include the doctors, nurses, cancer specialists, community teams, the Iain Rennie and Sue Ryder Hospices (and other similar havens), carers, administrative support teams, funeral directors and their teams, florists, crematorium staff and ministers. As someone who has worked in the field of Personal & Spiritual Development for more than 25 years, I am indebted to the work of these people who deal with the end of life.

Thank you to all who help us to die gracefully and with dignity.

Contents

An Introduction to Death and Dying

Attitudes and reactions to death and dying vary from culture to culture and from individual to individual. Even within families, where we might expect a similar response across family members as a result of genetic inheritance and conditioning, we see differences in how death and dying are approached and handled. What is behind these differences? Why is death truly celebrated in some cultures, with little or no sense of 'loss' and no 'grieving process' gone through, whilst in other cultures an appropriate period of time for 'mourning' is prescribed, irrespective of how any individual actually feels and where the grieving process is mapped out as if it is a psychological truth?

Some people advocate, and even insist on, black attire for funerals – which in many cultures is a symbol of menace or evil and is associated with unhappiness and formality – yet others wear a wide range of bright colours and choose informal dress codes. Is there a right way to deal with death? Is it right for us to throw ourselves into a state of depression, anger, sadness and guilt for months or even years on end? Is grieving really a mark of respect? Is it appropriate to be laughing, cheerful and happy at the funeral of a loved one or do we feel guilty for feeling positive about the situation? Our conditioned and 'human logic' responses will have the biggest impact on our own reactions unless we wake up to the fact that we are free to choose how we approach death and dying.

> *Human logic is very simply the way that we 'know' to do, think and feel and the meaning we give to our experiences. We are conditioned to follow a set of specific human logic rules.*

There really is no right or wrong way to handle death and dying. There are simply consequences for ourself and for others, based on the way in which we react and respond. It is to these consequences that we must give more attention, to ensure that we are living a truly fulfilled life, rather than simply accepting and following the conditioning and 'traditions' passed down to us, which may or may not be relevant or appropriate.

When you think about death and the process of dying what comes into your mind? What feelings do you have? When I was 18 years old I joined the Army. I served as a soldier and then an officer spanning a period of 12 years. Death didn't seem to have much relevance for me then. Yes, I was involved in armed conflict. Yes, I could have died, but for some reason it didn't seem to matter. I was wrapped up in the excitement and thrill of it all and I was blind to the consequences – not for me as I was aware that death would mean the absence of life – but for my family. I didn't harbour any thoughts of being a hero and dying that way. I simply didn't have any strong feelings about the idea of not being here! I was also, in some respects, fortunate not to have anyone significant to me die in my family until I was 29 years old, when my grandmother died following a heart attack at the age of 89. Her death caused me great pain and sadness for more than five years. It caused my mum great sadness over many more years and even though she became accustomed to the fact that her mother wasn't around to talk to, she always felt heartache as a result of Grandma's death. Mum had hoped to feel a connection with Grandma once she had gone and it was with a great sense of grief and loss that she was unable to experience that connection. I think it was more a case of Mum's expectations of what that connection should be like (hearing her voice, feeling her touch) that really let her down – her human logic idea of how things should be.

Of course, we all know death is the only thing we can guarantee in our lives and we know it will happen to those we love. What we often don't know is when and how it will happen. They say taxes are guaranteed too, but some people seem to avoid them! As I look back now, with my appreciation of Spiritual-Logic, which I will share with you throughout this book, I can 'see' exactly why I reacted the way I did to my grandmother's death, and why Mum struggled until her own, unexpected, death in 2011.

> *Spiritual-Logic is to 'see' beyond our human logic, that we have a choice about how we live*

our life, and to then make the choice that enables us to achieve our highest potential whilst also supporting others and the universe.

My grandmother's death had a huge impact on me. Perhaps it even shocked me into another reality about life? Following her death I used to wake in the night with a mild panicky sensation in my chest, close to my heart and stomach. Some might say this was because my heart was broken and I couldn't process (or literally stomach/digest) the death of my grandmother. What I do know was at that time I was also really thinking, in some detail, about death: my own death and the absolute reality that at some unknown point in time I would not exist. I simply would not be here to experience life. I put the anxiety response down to the fact that I was enjoying life so much that I didn't want it to end, which was true and fortunately enjoyment of life continues to be my reality. My logical mind was able to process the fact that if things went along as they should, the people of my own age that I know and love would be dying at about the same time too! But logic doesn't always override emotional responses that are so well conditioned. The anxiety decreased over time as I learned to accept my death would happen whether I wanted it to or not, as would the death of other loved ones. Fundamentally, I had to let go of my desire for control and address the idea of my own impermanence. With that letting-go came a new relationship with life and death and a different connection to the relationships I was involved in.

Human logic can't override emotional responses that are so well conditioned.

Of course, within our human logic rules we assume a certain hierarchy of death. Grandparents should go before their children, and our parents before we do. When this hierarchy is thrown out of sync it is easy to feel a sense of injustice on top of the loss, because we are conditioned to think our children dying before us is just not the way things should be. There are also the more subtle rules that we follow, such as 'the sick should go before the healthy' and more commonly 'bad people should go before good people'. If you have ever used the term 'they didn't deserve to die' then you too are following one of these subtle human logic rules, the consequences of which lead to an experience of unfairness. In turn this can result in the expression of anger, frustration, irritation, depression and guilt to name of the somewhat limiting emotional responses we are capable of. Our concept of 'fairness' is a human logic rule and not a Spiritual-Logic principle.

Even when we do have a hierarchy in our mind as to how things should play out, it doesn't always make the death of significant others easier to handle. For example, my grandmother dying at the age of 89 was actually harder for me to handle than my mother dying at the age of 72? Why was that the case? I loved and cared for them both equally and they were very precious and influential people in my life. For most people, handing the death of someone they love is one of the hardest things they ever have to handle – emotionally, mentally, physically and sometimes financially. Why is it that we struggle with the death of some people we are close to and not others? Sometimes we can struggle with family more than friends, sometimes the other way round. But not everyone struggles with death.

> *Achieving a positive, celebratory perspective on death and dying involves something other than religion or faith.*

Some people can accept death without anger and without guilt. Instead they rejoice and celebrate as if it were the birth of a healthy child, even when that death is the untimely death of their own child. Some might say that it is their religious belief or faith that helps them with acceptance, but that is not the case for everyone who is able to approach death in this way. Achieving a positive, celebratory perspective on death and dying involves something other than religion and faith.

We even mourn the death of people we don't know, as was the case with Princess Diana, who became the catalyst for British people (and others around the world) to openly express deep sadness following her unexpected death. Some said that her death gave people permission to express their own personal sadness – in respect of their own losses. This may be true, but the question is still, for what purpose do we need to express such sadness rather than celebration? Is our sadness an expression of celebration? Is Western society largely conditioned this way or is there another way? For what reason would we want to do it another way and is it necessary to do so? What is the problem with mourning death anyway? To answer these questions we need to appreciate the consequences for our own lives and of others we interact with.

For some people it is not the idea that they will die that causes them to experience negative emotions, but how they will die. One of the greatest challenges for some people during the process of dying (which can last hours, days, months or even years depending on where you consider the start point to be) is the loss of independence that results from a breakdown in either their body or mind. Sometimes we may have time to adjust to this loss of independence, become accustomed to it or, even better, to accept it. But often we may not have the time to adjust and may never accept it. Subsequently, the loss of independence can cause a great deal of distress to the person dying and those supporting them. Why then do we struggle to accept the help and support of others in such situations? Is it really our loss of independence that is the problem? Is our loss of independence simply an undeniable, unconscious, reminder of the fact that we are dying – however quickly or slowly that may be happening to us?

Why is it that some people are able to handle letting go more easily than others? Individual differences are often given as the justification for our responses to our experiences, yet when we really look at what is happening, it is the ingredients we put into our experience (the mental, emotional and spiritual ingredients), which are the difference that makes the difference – and there are common ingredients that generate specific outcomes. Firstly though, we need to know and understand those ingredients. Then we need to appreciate that we have control over the ingredients we put in. Then we can choose to make the changes we need in order to experience less distress, less anxiety, less loss, greater peace, celebration and acceptance in death and the process of dying.

Why is it that some people are able to handle letting go more easily than others?

Whatever your own approach to death and dying (or even to loss in a general sense), if you live in the western world, you are likely to be around people who do not handle death and dying in a way that supports their own development and the achievement of their highest potential. To have the ability to 'let go' without experiencing ongoing negative emotions: such as, sadness, anxiety, guilt, shame, anger and fear, whilst also remaining a compassionate, considerate, emotionally functional human being are qualities well worth developing. Spiritual-Logic is the process by which that becomes possible for you. It, like anything worth having in life, takes time, effort and dedication in order for you to become proficient. Being able to celebrate death and dying is not something that can be turned on when we want it – it is about developing our inner self through the application of Spiritual-Logic so that we can celebrate the death of others with compassion and joy… and most definitely without guilt and anger.

This book is for those people who would like to handle the death of their loved ones with a greater emphasis on celebration than mourning, and with greater compassion, love and acceptance than sadness, anger, stress and anxiety. It is also for those people supporting others going through the dying process, whether as a carer, or as the relative of a loved one. I also hope that you can take some of the lessons here and apply them to 'loss' in a general sense as this will result in a less stressful and more contented life.

The book can be read in a number of different ways. You can read it as a story from cover-to-cover and return to read the Spiritual-Logic Insights at a later date, or you can explore Spiritual-Logic within each chapter as you go through the story. You may choose to read just the latter part of the book, which starting from December 2010 chronicles the process of dying. You could, if you wished, just read the Developing Spiritual-Logic points for each section. However you approach reading this book, I hope that your journey provides all that you need to be able to appreciate and embrace a perspective that will help you to celebrate the death of loved ones and die peacefully and gracefully when your time comes.

What is Spiritual-Logic?

When we are conceived into this world we are pre-programmed to the environment in which we are intended to spend our early years. This pre-programming is, at the very least, a function of our genetic inheritance and our pre-natal experiences in the womb. When we are born, that programming continues through the teachings of our parents, our society and culture, our religions and governments, the media, our schooling and our social interactions. We are taught how to think, how to react to situations and how to cope with what life throws at us. Whether the things we are taught are in fact functional for us, support us, empower us, or not, we do not question. We are trained to think that the way we do things is the only way they are done and the right way.

> *We are trained to think that the way we do things is the only way they are done and the right way.*

We become identified with 'our way', which can then make change very challenging and even threatening for us. We mainly do this early learning by modelling ourselves on those around us. If we are fortunate enough to be surrounded by 'good' examples we are more likely to lead successful lives that contribute to the greater good of society. If we are surrounded by 'poor' examples, then our destiny may lead us to doing more of the same. You may have heard the phrase 'he didn't stand a chance', when referring to the upbringing of a young child in a dysfunctional family, if he is being sentenced for a criminal offence he has committed.

Although few would disagree as to what might be considered a right or wrong action within our society (we have lots of rules that help to shape our concept of right and wrong), when we begin to explore our world through our Spiritual-Logic, which is to see beyond our conditioning, things are not quite so black and white as we might wish. Through our Spiritual-Logic we must begin to question the human logic rules through which we were conditioned to think, feel and behave and take ourselves to a deeper level of self-awareness than we might feel comfortable experiencing. We must begin to question everything.

> *Engaging with our Spiritual-Logic means that we must begin to question everything.*

When we question, we must do so not for the purpose of being critical or dismissing something – this would be human logic in action. More importantly, we must question for the purpose of our personal and spiritual development and the attainment of our highest potential, success, contentment and inner peace. Living through the principles of Spiritual-

Logic leads us to be able to operate with greater levels of compassion for ourselves and others, become less judgmental, feel less stressed and to develop the highest levels of self-esteem. To engage with our Spiritual-Logic is to wake up to our lives so that we can take personal responsibility rather than blaming others (including our dysfunctional upbringing) and in so doing we become able to see that change really is a choice.

Anything less than engaging with our Spiritual-Logic, anything less than waking up to our lives is to live through the history of others and remain within the constraints of our habitual upbringing and narrow-minded thinking. Developing our Spiritual-Logic takes effort and exposes us to aspects of ourself we would probably rather not wake up to, but it is only through this waking that we are truly able to assert our will (volition) and live our own lives in a way that is also supportive of others and the universe. Through the process of Spiritual-Logic we begin to see inside our soul and our connection to the souls of others. We break the illusions of human logic that constrain our ability to truly connect with others and we begin to feel an unlimited sense of personal freedom, peace and contentment.

Just to be clear, many people have their own interpretation of what is meant by the term 'spiritual'. There are spiritual or Universal Laws, there are spiritual churches and there are people who label themselves as 'spiritual'. Some say it is different things to different people, but what they are really referring to when they talk in this way is the human logic idea of 'spiritual'. Spiritual-Logic is not about any religion or specific faith. It is not specific to any individual interpretation, group or culture. It is our engagement with an aspect of our human capability and functioning and therefore it is possible for anyone to learn and adopt, should they wish to. You may already be living, at least in part, through your Spiritual-Logic, perhaps without realizing it.

> *Spiritual-Logic is our highest level of human functioning.*

When one of my clients was asked, 'Why Spiritual-Logic?' she said, 'Because it makes sense.' And it does. It is a method of awakening to our true potential, by recognising the reality of our human conditioning and its impact on our ability to live happy and fulfilling lives.

> *If human logic is the problem, then Spiritual-Logic is the solution.*

In this book I have taken a case study very close to my own heart and shared my discoveries and appreciation of Spiritual-Logic along the way. It is the story of my mother's last few months of life. This is Mum's story, it is my story and it is the story of many other people. During the last few months of Mum's life she said to me, 'this would make a great story, you have to write it.' So I have. I have written it in the hope that it helps other people: the families and friends of those who discover suddenly, as we did, that someone they love will die within a short period of time; for those in the caring industry supporting us all; and for those who are taking the final part of their journey to everlasting peace. The events here are all true. The human logic interpretation is of course through my own experience of these events. If one of my siblings had written this, or indeed my mother, then the interpretation would be different. Spiritual-Logic is explored and demonstrated throughout the case study, written in italics to differentiate it from the main text and at the end of each chapter there are Spiritual-Logic Insights and Developmental Points.

My hope is to bring to you a new level of awareness, or even reinforce your own intuitive thinking, in a way that helps you or others should you experience a similar situation. Since we all have to handle loss, and dying is one aspect of loss, then I hope you will take the principles within this book and apply them across the broader spectrum of your life too.

A New Beginning

On the 3rd February 1939 a very special little baby girl was born to two exceptional people. Of course there are many special babies born every day to exceptional people, but only one of them turned out to be my mother, born to my grandparents, Gracie and Lesley. That wonderful baby, my mum and mum to my brother and twin sisters, died on 20th September 2011 aged 72 years, following the diagnosis of a brain tumour in March of that same year.

Named Valerie Irene Eunice Porter, Mum entered the world just before war broke out, so her formative years living on the outskirts of London were, like many children of that time, tough. She had a brother, Dick, who was three years older than her. Mum's early experiences of rationing, blackouts, sirens and the constant threat of being bombed had an impact that would last a lifetime. At four years old Mum recounted a visit to Brighton to see her mum's older sister, Aunt Lil. They didn't visit Brighton that often because the cost and time it took precluded such visits, so the one time Mum did go should have been a special event. On that specific day though, Brighton was bombed. Mum told her story of hiding under the kitchen table shaking like a leaf and when it had all died down she stepped outside to see that the house just four doors down was rubble. Needless to say they did not visit Brighton again during those war years.

Mum was a very quiet and shy young girl. She was bought up with strong morals and values, which you would expect in the post-Victorian era: respect, honesty, integrity, family, love and loyalty to name just a few. She went to church as a young child and also to a school that was strongly influenced by the church. She described her experiences of both church and school as 'putting the fear of God into you'. The vicar conducting the service on a Sunday morning would put so much energy and passion into his sermon that the front row would walk out covered in spittle. Heaven and Hell were very real concepts about which Mum and I had a number of debates some years later. She never frequented church on a regular, or even irregular, basis during her adult years, but her faith in her God was present throughout her life. Mum was also frightened to death of the head teacher at her school who was so big that when she sat in her car it would visibly tilt to one side. So as a small and quiet child, Mum felt intimidated by both the vicar and the head. I suspect that this was the case with many young girls being schooled at that time. It was certainly indicative of the culture of the time and the fear-based approach that was prevalent.

S-L

Fear plays a huge role in our lives. It can be helpful when alerting us to a real danger, but when fear is used for the purpose of control (as it most often is) it inhibits our development, reduces our options, kills our spirit and leads us into narrow-mindedness. Fear motivates us, but it doesn't inspire us.

Whilst there are many supportive values and principles we can take from our religions and faiths, there are also many interpretations of those religions that preclude other's, or promote other's as being less than one's own. The idea of Heaven and Hell and other promises made by religions are actually those of human logic and primarily for the purpose of control of behaviour. We fear the threat or fall for the promise of a better world and behave accordingly. Do we really need such controls in order to live a conscientious life that also supports the higher potential of others?

Sadly, Mum's early schooling experiences had a significant impact on her desire for learning for some years. She openly admitted to having a fear of learning that she put down to her experiences throughout her school days. It is somewhat ironic that I, her eldest daughter, spent my career in a teaching capacity, as a physical training instructor in the Army and then as a personal development coach and mentor. I was both Mum's antagonist and her soulmate in this respect. I spent many years sharing my knowledge with Mum on a wide range of things, from running a marathon to playing golf, and at the end using visual imagery to help her with the tumour. She would listen, argue, reflect and then at some point, sometimes a few months down the line I would find her regurgitating things I had said. She always used to justify my knowledge as 'common sense' rather than science and she was of course right. Most personal development training and coaching is common sense. It's just that sometimes we need to teach common sense. I always used to say that she knew everything I did. It was just that my knowledge had come mostly from books and hers through personal experience. She agreed with that and I always learned from her because, of course, real life experiences are our reality, no matter what the book says!

In spite of Mum's open fear, thankfully, she did not stop learning. Mum was a naturally inquisitive individual always keen to know why something was the way it was and she always relished a challenge. She was more pragmatic than academic, so she would literally be able to turn her hand to anything. She had a love of history and the sciences, at which she had been good at school. While her early adult years were taken up with bringing up a family, which happened twice really as there are ten years between my brother and I and my twin sisters, she later found great solace and entertainment in that modern day invention – the television and specifically Sky Digital. Mum would spend a great deal of time absorbed in the History and Natural Science programmes and they kept her entertained throughout the winter months in her later life. Whilst in the hospice in the last few weeks of her life she would avidly watch the nature programmes and specifically the series chronicling the lives of a 'mob' of meerkats.

S-L

Learning is a natural and fundamental aspect of being human. It is how we create, influence, grow and develop and of course how we survive – to deny someone of it, to stall it or inhibit it in oneself, in any way, is to deny our Soul food. The result of such treatment can only lead to a diminished sense of Spirit and Self – let alone if we then consider the impact on others of the ignorance that must follow. Learning must be appreciated in its broadest and purest sense, rather than through the institutionalised systems of control that we call our educational establishments – which are, for the most part, not actually about learning so much as conditioning.

As a young child Mum's life was poor, but at the same time rich. Her family didn't have much money, many possessions or even food at times. During her last months, as she reflected on her life, Mum recalled feeling hungry for most of her young teenage years. Her family could hardly be described as successful by today's materialistic standards. What they did have though, which is missing for many young people these days, was the real 'richness' of life. They were able to play safely in the streets, venture into the woods, climb trees, pick berries and fruits, entertain themselves without purchased toys, make things from nature, and learn the art of embracing all that is natural in life. They had a quality of life that most people now can only dream of. Mum talked of the many times that they would all go berry picking in the woods at the weekend with their close neighbours, as one big family unit. They would eat as much as they could and pick the rest. Some would be used for jam and some would make pies. This was a family unit that would span a lifetime, with one of Mum's longest and closest friends, Denny, who was born next door to mum and who lived for the last 30 years just two doors down from her. They were like sisters, sharing their own family lives with each other over the years in the way their mothers had done before them.

> *It is engaging in the simple pleasures of nature that adds the greatest value to our lives and to the lives of others.*

Mum may have been shy, but she was also strong-willed. Most people who knew her in her later years would describe her as a feisty character. She also had a strong sense of right and wrong, not only in respect of the law and rules, but also in the need to be right and not be wrong. As a young child though she would, as we all have done, break the rules – in her case, ever so gently. Her mum and dad went out one day leaving her in the competent hands of her older brother and cousin. It was a cold day and there was ice on the canal. Mum of course saw this as an opportunity to walk where you cannot normally walk. As a child being told not to walk on the ice is, as any parent knows, like saying walk on the ice. In spite of her brother repeatedly telling Mum not to walk on the ice she couldn't resist the temptation. Her inquisitive nature took over, just to see what happens if… and, yes, the ice gave way. She was duly pulled out by her brother and cousin, marched home, stripped and dried by the fire. It is wonderful to think of my mother as a child doing the things we all do as children. As her child I of course did not know her then and when you're growing up you don't always get to see the child in your parents. They may play with you for a bit, but their world is all wrapped up in seriousness, work, money and other such adult ventures!

One Christmas Mum and Dick woke to find small boxes at the bottom of their beds. Both had been given the same size box, wrapped in the same paper and making the same rattling sound when shaken. Mum looked at Dick somewhat bemused. There must have been a mistake. How could they both have the same toy for Christmas? They quickly opened their presents. Dick was delighted at his box of toy soldiers. Mum less so! She was beside herself with the injustice.

> *We have a strong human logic sense of what constitutes justice and right or wrong, but that doesn't necessarily mean others agree with us.*

Her parents must have got it wrong. So she marched into their bedroom and demanded to know where her present was, because she had just opened a present that was clearly not for her but for her brother. Her mum and dad tried to explain that they had wanted to give them both the same thing in order to be fair. Mum's response was to say that she shouldn't be getting toy soldiers because she was a girl. This sense of stereotypical right and wrong was something she endeavoured (unsuccessfully) to instil in her children. I was such a disappointment to her in this respect. As a child, I hated pink, hated dresses, hated dollies and wanted a football! It took me 13 years to get that football, but it was worth the fight. I was the antithesis of Mum's expectations of a daughter. Mum couldn't believe how many of her rules I broke, something that would cause her much pain along the way, but much joy in the end. Perhaps her mum and dad were, without knowing it, preparing Mum for what was to come with her own children, or perhaps this is just the natural cycle of human logic.

S-L

We forget that our parents were children – we even forget that we were once children and as a result our life can become very serious and intense, which may be our interpretation of what it means to grow up. Maintaining the positive childlike qualities of curiosity, trust, innocence, exploration, adventure, boundary-pushing, non-judgmentalism and joy is essential for our Spirit to thrive. What have you done lately, that has fully expressed your childlike qualities and made your Spirit soar with joy?

Mum, like many young women of that era, left school at 15. By this time her brother had joined the RAF and was away from home. In fact he was away from home for the next 35 years give or take a few 'flying visits'! When Mum was 14 their father died from a heart condition: a condition that would have been easily treatable today. Mum remembered her father as being poorly virtually all her life. She never got to play with him as one would hope to with their dad. She had to sit quietly, help nurse him and not create too much of a disturbance. Mum said he was a kind, loving and warm-hearted man. I know she missed the presence of her dad a great deal in her young life. Gracie, her mum worked at this time at the local record factory in order to support the family. Mum had always wanted to be a draughtswoman. In all honesty it would have really suited her desire for straight lines and detail. She was very precise, particularly concerning cleanliness and tidiness. She would have loved the exactness of the draughtswoman's work, but because they needed the money she could not take up an apprenticeship. Instead, she joined her mother at the local record factory. The money was better, especially as it was piecework – and she was an exceptionally conscientious worker.

Maybe working at the record factory is where Mum's love of music developed. She never did say. Her school report definitely didn't indicate any love or appreciation of music since it was one of her worst subjects! Yet, Mum really did love music. She had quite a good voice too and would love singing to us when we were young children. She had an eclectic taste in music, from Meat Loaf to Josh Groban, The Pogues' Christmas song to *Fiddler on the Roof*. I think the common factors in Mum's taste came down to it needing to sound great and have relatable lyrics. She also enjoyed The Spinners, John Denver, *Joseph*, *Les Miserables*, *The Phantom of the Opera*, *Swan Lake*, Eva Cassidy, Country & Western, Folk, Jazz and Blues. In fact, she probably enjoyed a bit of everything, except those things I enjoyed as a teenager! She was okay with The Beatles, but when we hit the 70s and 80s she decided that the music wasn't music anymore. It was just a loud noise. She was of course right from her perspective... and I can safely predict that I will say the same thing to my daughter when she hits her teens. After all, that's what mums do!

Spiritual-Logic Insights

To engage with our Spiritual-Logic is to recognise our conditioning for what it is. It is designed for our survival. It sets us up so that we can evolve our life. It provides the foundations upon which we can either build our tower of strength or become a wilting lily. Whether we consider our conditioning to be supporting our life or inhibiting it is a judgment that only we can decide for ourselves, the deciding of which will either support or inhibit us! Neither is in fact true. It just is what it is and we have the power to create our future on the back of it.

Our conditioning, then, is a set of conditions within which we have been raised, no more and no less. They may not have been the conditions we would have chosen for ourselves, but it has happened the way it has and we cannot change the past or our genetic inheritance. We are like a cake that is being baked with a specific set of ingredients and as we grow we can make a choice to change the ingredients, so that eventually we may have the cake we want. Or we can of course maintain the same ingredients, then accept and learn to appreciate ourself as we are. To think of ourself as powerless to change something that we do not like (in ourself) and to reject ourself for not being good enough, is to fall foul of our human logic and will set us up for a life of misery and discontent.

One reason our personal and spiritual development is so important is because it provides us with a wider range of further ingredients to use (thoughts, behaviours and emotional responses). It enables us to create Wisdom within us that we can draw upon to effectively navigate the stormier waters during our life. This, then, enables us to offer the best of ourselves under a wider range of external conditions, for our own benefit as well as for the benefit of others. Anything less than this is truly selfish.

Developing Spiritual-Logic

- ✓ Start to question, for the purpose of awakening yourself, the very foundations you thought were true – your conditioned human logic.

- ✓ Really 'look' at your parents or significant others (even if they have already died). Give compassion for any aspects of their behaviours, rules, attitudes, etc. that you don't like – they are the product of their conditioning too and remember that you are also a part of them!

- ✓ Embrace all aspects of your life for what they bring to you now, and know that you can change the ingredients, if you allow yourself to. If you don't feel able to change the ingredients, accept yourself as being the best of 'you' that you can be.

- ✓ If you feel threatened by another's perspective, remember you don't have to agree with it – you simply acknowledge that it is as valid as yours, and that it is right for them in that moment in time.

- ✓ Look for the ways in which your upbringing has inspired you to be where you are now.

Marriage and Family

Mum fell in love early in her life and was married at just 19, in October 1958. Gracie had married late and gave birth to Mum when she was 33, so she definitely didn't follow in her mum's footsteps on the marriage front. But Mum had met her prince and she was deeply in love with him. He was to become our father. They had a stillborn baby two years before I came along, which was heartbreaking. Mum's main love in life, apart from my father at that time, was children. She had always wanted children and she had a very good way with them: firm and loving. Although Mum didn't speak of the death of her baby that often, I know it was something she never really came to terms with. Perhaps you can't come to terms with something like that. Perhaps you just have to learn to live with it. I know this caused her a great deal of pain, especially because she was unable to speak to anyone about it at the time. Counselling was not readily available then and my father was of strict Victorian principles. Mum was told adamantly not to cry and to get on with it.

S-L

When we suppress our self-expression – even if that self-expression is the pain we are feeling – we cause ourselves great internal suffering, which is unnecessary and can contribute to illness and impact on our body's ability to heal. To deny another person such expression (however unwittingly) is to violate their Soul development.

Mum was not used to hiding her feelings in this way. She had been brought up in an environment where it was okay to communicate and share how you felt. She was conditioned to appreciate sickness and vulnerability so she was emotionally empathic and, what I would call, connected. My father on the other hand was in many respects the opposite. He was conditioned with strict rules that said you didn't show your feelings or any vulnerability at any time, to anyone – not even your wife.

> *When we suppress our self-expression we cause ourself great internal suffering.*

I think this single difference between them was to be the root of many problems along their journey together. I do believe my father was an emotionally sensitive man, and I often said that to Mum. She was not so convinced, partly because she could only see the pain he caused her. Dad turned to alcohol, maybe as early as the death of his first baby girl, or maybe even before he met Mum. In any event the dates don't really matter. Alcohol was to contribute to the death of their relationship and eventually at the age of 66 it killed my father.

S-L

There is an addictive or obsessive nature in us all. Sometimes this nature is directed towards external substances, sometimes to our need for control, or power, sometimes to our negativity and problems, sometimes to our work or sporting activities. It is this nature (of more and excess) that also drives us to achieve, improve and develop ourselves. It is therefore an aspect of our desire and passion – without which we would lead soulless human lives.

Addictive substances are used as an escape from a world that we are struggling to navigate, and it has been said that they help us achieve a similar state of oblivion and connection as that achieved by those who meditate. As far as I know though, no-one has ever died from meditation!

Mum gave birth to me in November 1963. She was in labour for 24 hours. When the nurse who had gone off shift the night before came in the next morning she was astounded to see Mum still going, exhausted and not much further forward than when she had left her the night before. Mum said, 'what did they expect, having lost my first baby at birth I didn't want to let you come out.' It is interesting that I felt for many years, on many levels, that Mum didn't want to let go of me. I am sure most parents struggle with letting their children grow up, leave home and make their own choices, but our connection was a strong one that challenged me at times. Even now I still feel there is a big part of us that is inseparable, connected, in a very positive and supportive way.

Mum gave birth to my brother in December 1964. This is a tough challenge in parenting, having two children with just a year between them. We lived in a very small cottage at the time. Everything was hand-washed and dried if the weather permitted. Mum still used a mangle to wring the clothes out. Housekeeping and looking after two small children without all the mod cons was a full time 24/7 job by anyone's standards. Mum, of course, brought us up with the same strict house rules that she was raised with. In such a confined environment and with the physical hardship that she had to endure just for us to survive this is understandable. You need to run a tight ship for things to function, let alone function smoothly. Mum was an advocate of 'a tidy house is a tidy mind'. She had a strong sense of personal pride and would not want anyone to be able to say that she didn't look after her family. She looked after us very well and protected us from things that parents should protect their children from. She was not overly controlling, nor did she ever try to be my friend, she simply operated the home with strict rules and gave us lots of love.

In fact, these are the common parental standards that make for grounded and well-adjusted children and subsequently, healthy functioning adults. From a psychological perspective she did an excellent job without any university degree. She used to tell me the story of Dr Spock, who wrote many books on child development that were popular in her parenting era. Mum said that having written the books he subsequently, some years later, openly admitted that he was wrong. I am not sure if it is true, but she laughed a lot about that because it seemed to sum up her recognition that just because something is written doesn't make it true. Wise words. Mum was very astute and intuitive – something that didn't come from her schooling.

S-L

There is a fine line between boundaries set for the purpose of providing an appropriate and safe environment for a developing child, in which the child will thrive, and boundaries for the purpose of control, driven by one's own fears and unhealthy needs, which leads to rigidity and dysfunction. The deciding factor is the 'intention' (the purpose or mental aim) of the person putting in place those boundaries, which can only be appreciated when you have a deeper understanding of yourself. 'Intention' in this context is to say our 'underlying motivations and drivers', which may reside in our unconscious or conditioned past – which means we may not be aware of our 'true intention' unless we have a higher sense of self-awareness.

Mum had always wanted three children. She had dreamed of it as a young woman. Some women seem to have these things mapped out in their minds: marriage, children, house. Now, she was pregnant again and very happy as her grand plan was realising itself. You can imagine her surprise when, about seven months into her pregnancy, she found out she was having twins. That wasn't in the plan! I remember the day she found out because we were with Dad in the local outdoor swimming pool and Mum waddled in and sat down. She looked shocked. I was overjoyed at the idea of two brothers or sisters. I clearly had no idea of the consequences or workload involved, but I think my joy and excitement might have helped balance her shock. I am not sure how my brother felt. He was always quite a quiet chap and I was too into my world to know what was going on in his. I have no idea how my dad felt about the idea of two more children, either, or even if any more children were in his plan. He never said. He just carried on working to provide for his family.

The twins were born on 17th July 1974, just four minutes apart. Mum was now over her need to 'hold on' and couldn't wait for them to arrive. Her labour was just a few hours and the delivery process was a very quick one. The twins weighed in at about 4lbs so they were put into intensive care. Mum was in hospital for a few days. The twins had to stay a bit longer, so Mum would walk up and down the hill several times a day to be with them. I remember when they eventually came home. Jakk would have her eyes open, what seemed like most of the time and Nat would sleep, literally like a baby. They were fascinating to watch. Their every movement enthralled me. I always thought I got any maternal instinct out of me as a result of my experiences with my little sisters. Little did I know that these instincts would return with the planning and birth of my own daughter at the age of 46. We should never under-estimate the potential for something we hadn't planned to transform our life! During the summer holidays I shared the feeding and changing routines with Mum during the night. I don't remember much else about that summer, except feeling exhausted and happy. Mum was weary and seemed to be working all hours. Still doing odd jobs (that could be done from home) to make ends meet, endless washing and drying (especially towelling nappies) and cooking and cleaning. It was a full-time job before with two children, now it was a full-time job for more than one person. At least we had a washing machine by then, a twin tub. We still relied on the weather for drying though. One thing Mum prided herself on was always having a meal for us. Given her early experiences of hunger she was determined that we never went hungry. She did a great job on all fronts. We always had food on the table, clean clothes and a tidy house.

> *We should never under-estimate the potential for something we hadn't planned to transform our life.*

When the twins were very young they contracted whooping cough. Today they vaccinate against this dreadful illness. As anyone knows who has had to nurse a child with whooping cough, it is a life and death situation. It was a 24-hours-a-day nursing job for Mum. I was taken into hospital at this time, for a week, because I had a flu virus and Mum simply couldn't cope with two very sick babies and an unwell child. She gave every ounce of herself to take care of my sisters. On two occasions one of them stopped breathing and Mum resuscitated them back to life. She was exhausted, but she never left their side night after night, day after day. I cannot remember how long they were ill for, but it seemed like a very long time to an 11-year-old. The doctor remarked that they would never have survived without Mum's dedicated attention. There were no lengths Mum wouldn't go to protect her children. They were her purpose in life.

In April 1984 Mum and Dad were officially divorced. The process had taken a couple of years. During this time we had all moved back out to Mum's birth village and closer to her mum. I do believe that both my parents wanted their marriage to work and they fought to make that happen in their own way. The problem was that their ways of fighting for it seemed to make matters worse. On one occasion Mum asked Dad to move out of our house, so she could get some space. He wouldn't, so we trekked up the road to my grandma's house with all our belongings and moved in with her. He didn't want the family to split up and Mum couldn't live with him anymore. Eventually he did move out and we moved back down the road to our house. This period of time had taken its toll on Mum, but her strength and determination grew and grew. I think to be honest she had reached rock bottom and, if you want to live, there is only one place you can go from there.

If you want to live, there is only one place you can go when you have hit rock bottom.

She was determined to make a life for herself and her children. My brother and I were 17 and 18 respectively when the divorce finally came through so we were starting to live a bit more independently. They sold the house and Mum moved into a small two-up, two-down cottage in the village, where she was to live out the rest of her life. Dad moved into the main town and lived in his own place, until he died. Mum lived just a couple of doors down from her best friend, Denny, who she lived next door to as a child. She worked hard to pay the mortgage and give as much as she could to her children to ensure they did not go hungry or without.

S-L

Two people may be joined by marriage, which is of human logic design, but the reality is that we are joined energetically. Soulmates don't always get on together. Soulmates are there to help each other evolve, which can mean conflict. At some point in time, though, if the two energies are going in different directions, perhaps because the timing isn't right, it is the right time to let go and move on. Blame is not needed or desired, because blame comes from our fears and does nothing but harm. What is necessary is to give love and respect, to appreciate our own contribution to the situation and to forgive ourself, and others, for not providing fully for our needs.

In June 1984, just two months after the divorce was finalised, I left home and joined the Army. This, initially, destroyed Mum as it wasn't in her mind for me to leave. She had spent her life living so close to her mum and it was natural to think (or hope) that I would do the same. At the time, though, I knew that I had to get away. I had to get a break from the previous years of stress and sadness. I remember I had a lot of angry feelings back then. What better way to express them than dodging bombs on the streets of Northern Ireland! The idea of going on an adventure appealed to me, but I still cried all the way on the bus to Guildford and on and off for many years. My connection with my mother was so strong and the thought of being responsible for more sadness in her saddened me greatly. My leaving though was a good thing, and necessary, for Mum too. Sometimes our children teach us things and it is important to always be open to that possibility. She had relied on me a great deal ever since the twins were born and particularly over the period of the divorce and I think when I left she, like me, knew she had to focus on carving out a new life. She was just 45 years old and had been married 26 of those years, with the expectation of that relationship lasting forever. But now, she could see a new future. It would of course be different from her original expectations, but it was one that held with it the hope of a happy and fulfilled life. Mum became more independent, perhaps because she had to, but she was also good at it. She was strong-willed, determined and she knew she could fend for herself and her family.

Sometimes our children teach us things and it is important to always be open to that possibility.

Spiritual-Logic Insights

To engage with our Spiritual-Logic is to learn to effectively express our inner voice. This involves us aligning with our true self, which also means to accept our conditioned past for what it is rather than wishing we were someone else. We may enter into relationships with others, because this is our need, but that doesn't mean that we should compromise our sense of Self or our Soul along the way.

Marriage is a human social construction, it is not of our Spirit. Unity with others is inherent in our co-existence. Our Souls connect without the need for ritual and the approval of others. Sometimes we ignore this Soul connection because the relationship falls outside of our socially expected norms. This is done at great cost to our Spirit. Our human logic failing is not to see such rituals for what they are. Today's increasingly commercial approach to the union between two people doesn't prevent us from continuing to pursue a path of separation with them. Sometimes this separation take place within our marriage – through power struggles, competitive behaviour and our desire to control. These are all a function of our inherent inadequacy, our fears and our ego's desire and need to feel that we are 'special'.

Rituals play a strong role in our psyche, but the internal ritual – driven by Spirit rather than the one driven by our ego is the one to tune into. In nature we see a wide range of relationships across species – some mate for life, others are based on procreation alone. In some the females control the relationship, in others it is the male. They don't need pieces of paper to validate them and there are no tax benefits for them to do things in a particular way. Have we put ourselves above animals in formalising the union between two people, or have we simply stifled our Soul expression for the purpose of social convention?

In our social interactions we may expect others to provide for our needs, but we must also appreciate the boundaries within which they are able to operate. They are not perfect and neither are we. The only person who can truly provide for your needs is you.

Developing Spiritual-Logic

✓ Recognise the impermanence of your relationships. Whether death is the thing that separates you, or you go your own separate ways in life, they will always come to an end.

✓ Celebrate your relationships for what they are and what you bring to them, without expecting perfection.

- ✓ Ensure your boundaries are for the purpose of safety and security rather than control and paranoia.
- ✓ Follow your Soul connection rather than social convention. Do not compromise your Soul – no matter what it takes. To do so is to fall out of alignment with your Self, which can only lead to regret. Tune in to your Self to know whether you are a slave to your ego's desires.
- ✓ When a relationship comes to its natural end, let it go – with love and gratitude.

Creating a New Life

Over the next few years Mum started to regain her confidence and carve out her new life, including learning to drive, running a half marathon, taking up golf and getting into her gardening. Yes life was hard, especially in the early days, but Mum was one very determined woman and there was never any doubt that she would make the best of the situation she was in. Mum started running to get fit and put herself in for a half marathon at 50. She was, rightly, so proud of her achievement having never done anything like it before, and so was I. It lifted her spirits and made her realise she could do whatever she set her sights on. She was strong-minded and decided, albeit a bit reluctantly, that she would also give up smoking. She turned to Nicorette to help her. She certainly never smoked a cigarette again in her life, but the Nicorette was never far from her handbag, especially in the last few months of her life.

She also got herself a car. Initially, she went for a little run around with a small engine, but later she decided to get something with a bit of zip in it! She loved the acceleration and transformed into Sterling Moss at times, with a little road rage thrown in when other drivers got in her way. Being able to drive gave her a new-found freedom – and vocal expression (mostly swearing!) – although she was never that keen on motorways and especially the M25. On one occasion she went over to Essex to visit a friend. On her return journey she got on the M25 – about half way round and just before the exit she could have taken to get home, she realised she was going around it the wrong way (compared to her journey there). So she came off and got back on it going in the opposite direction. By the time she got home more than three hours later she had travelled right around the M25, twice!

The car was convenient and the marathon a personal challenge. Both were a turning point in respect of Mum starting to do things just for herself – which is no mean feat for someone who has spent their life dedicated to their children. Golf though was to become her passion, her inspiration and her life… and she got good at it.

Those who know golf know that you either love it or hate it. Mum became obsessive about golf. She watched it, talked about it, practiced it and played it. She even dreamt golf! I knew golf, so she used me as her coach, which meant I got lots of phone calls when her round hadn't gone as she thought it should. She was never a long hitter of the ball. She had not played a great deal of sports in her youth and didn't have a natural appreciation of the physics of these things, but she was very good at following instructions. So, because of this she got herself a tidy swing and most often the ball went straight down the middle. Because length was an issue for her she learned to master the short game. We had lots of fun practicing different types of short game shots. She loved playing the floating lob shot (even though it is far more challenging than the chip and run) and she seemed to have a knack of getting that ball close to the hole from 50 yards into the green. She also developed a mean putting stroke. Fearlessly she would putt and more often than not she was very successful. She loved her short game, even though she still would complain about the length of her drives at times (and particularly in the winter). She loved the finesse and precision dictated by the short game. It fit with her desire for detail and intricacy. Very simply, she loved and lived golf!

Motivation is of the mind, Inspiration is of our Soul.

Throughout the 15 years that Mum played golf she always strived to improve. Every year she would decide she wanted to learn something new and would work on a wide range of short game shots. Mum won some major competitions at her club and she was one of only three golfers to win the Bailey Crystal 36-hole tournament two years in succession. Every year she talked about making that tournament hers once again. That was by far her most prized win and something she was, rightly, so proud of.

S-L

Inspiration is a Soul food and if we feel inspired to do something then we need to make sure we do it, providing we don't harm another in the process. Being inspired to improve creates high vibrational energy and quality action. Inspiration is far more powerful than motivation because motivation is of our mind and inspiration is of our Soul. You can literally feel the difference.

Mum played competitive golf until she became ill. She played mixed competitions and for various teams for the ladies' section of the club. She would share everything she had learned with her golfing partners and she was someone they enjoyed playing with. The most common comment I have heard from her club members is 'she always inspired me to keep going'. But golf was more than a fun game to Mum. It was a mental challenge, a physical exercise and a social outlet. She initially loved golf for the challenge and in the last couple of years the social aspects had become more important to her. The ladies were her main social life. She would love chatting to them, having a laugh and putting the world to rights. I will be forever grateful that Mum had this wonderful outlet for her retirement.

Mum's other love was her garden. She got more and more into gardening over the last few years. She had a long garden of about 180ft and sectioned it off. She built a Japanese themed area at the house end, and a vegetable garden and fruit bushes at the top end, and grass separated the two areas. She loved going to garden centres to find things that would fit her vision for the garden. She knew what would work and if she didn't see it she wouldn't buy for the sake of it. Even when she did see something she wanted she would be very cautious about spending that much money on something for the garden. I would always urge her to buy because her garden gave her so much pleasure. Mum spent hours in her garden. She had a small section of plants that she called Grandma's plants (her mother Gracie). These were old country plants that you may not find too many of these days. She had taken them from Grandma's garden after she died. They kept Mum in touch with her mother, which is something that was very important to her. Mum told me once that she was very sad that since her mother had died she had never felt the connection with her that she had expected to. Mum would talk to her mum all the time, but it upset her that she never felt as if she was hearing her mother speak to her, which was what she wanted. She felt she had lost something very dear to her (which of course she had). This connection did return to Mum, later.

Spiritual-Logic Insights

To engage with our Spiritual-Logic is not to under-estimate our potential. If we are too caught up in our conditioned past we continue to handle life through the limitations imposed on us instead of realising that we have the capacity for greatness.

If you think the way you are is fixed, then accept that and get the best out of yourself that you can. If you want to change, then seek out how to do it and make it happen. Anything less than that is to fail yourself.

Taking strength from our resilience to past adversities that we have overcome enables us to know that we are capable of carving out a future of our own design. We may not know this until later, but as soon as we become aware of our strength it is the right time to exercise it. Doing things to improve ourself is an essential aspect of developing high self-esteem, since we can then perceive ourself to be competent. It also leads to us being able to offer a greater contribution in life and thereby develop the sense of a life well spent.

The feeling of inspiration is a great source of food for our Soul. It lightens our life, gives us great energy and connects us to our Spirit. We live in a world full of inspiration should we wish to see it: nature, other people, our connection to something far greater than us, our faith, our religion, and of course our life and what we do. The energy of inspiration is strong, but we have to open our eyes to see it and open our mind to feel it.

When we really connect with nature we become at one with something that is far bigger and far greater than we are. This doesn't mean that we need to learn to love gardening, or get a pet! We simply need to give respect to nature and appreciate the value it brings to our world. This connection to the natural world is a link to our inherent oneness, which means our spirit has come home. There is a great deal of comfort and a sense of inner peace that comes from this connection.

Developing Spiritual-Logic

- ✓ Inspiring other people inspires ourself. It connects us as one and has the power to move mountains, should we wish to do so.
- ✓ Look for your parent's/significant other's strengths. Don't be undermined or intimidated by them because that would be a poor choice. Instead rejoice in the fact that you too have infinite potential, should you choose to exercise it.
- ✓ Take a walk in nature or even watch it on the television and absorb yourself in its magnificence, whilst also holding on to the fact that you are a part of this wonder of the world.
- ✓ Accept if it is time for you to move on and take the leap. Trust in your own abilities to come through any storm, stronger and more confident than when you entered it.
- ✓ See every experience as an opportunity to learn about yourself and your connection with others. Do not feel threatened by this journey. Instead, feel excited about your discoveries because they will lead you to a more empowered and contented life. What have you learned today?

Becoming a Grandmother at Last!

Mum was not a drinker but we had a 70th birthday party for her at our cousin's house and she partook in a celebration drink. Mum's brother, Dick, brought with him several bottles of Bollinger champagne. Mum always loved the idea of champagne but never got to drink it that often. At Christmas we used to have cheap fizzy with orange juice in it, so Bollie was a real treat. Mum took to it like a duck to water... She never got drunk but she was certainly very merry on this occasion. She declared that now she was 70 it was time to let go of her maternal role, let her (now grown-up) children get on with their own lives, and she was going to start to learn about the internet and how to use email. Mum declared all her children released! She had been given a laptop for her birthday to facilitate this new desire to learn and she proceeded to explore the World Wide Web. Of course she never did let go of those maternal instincts, she continued to worry about her children and voice her opinion just as openly as she had since we were born... and she never did get to grips with email and the World Wide Web either!

It was around this time that Murielle and I decided that we were going to have children. Murielle was going to be the birth mother, but Mum embraced the fact that she was going to be a grandmother. Her desire to be a grandmother overrode any challenges she had in respect of the lack of a conventional method of achieving it. Being a grandmother was everything that Mum had ever wanted or dreamed of since having four of her own children. Most importantly, there was the Grannies' Cup to play for at her golf club! She joked every year that she was the oldest person in the non-grannies version of the cup. Although she joked, I know it was something she was deeply saddened by. So the news that she would be a grandmother delighted her.

S-L

To truly accept different perspectives to be as valid as your own is the essence of Wisdom. Wisdom, then, comes from, not least, a flexibility of mind, a non-judgmental attitude and the giving of unconditional love.

Before Amelie was born we decided to have a baby shower. We decided on a spiritual baby shower. 'What is that?' said mum. 'Sounds a bit strange to me.' I was always introducing her to 'spiritual things', such as the idea of past lives, spirits, energy healing and quantum psychology. She tolerated me well. I talked as if I had just invented these things and of course she knew they had been around forever. Sometimes there was no difference in what I was preaching as the way to live life, and the old wives' tales that were told over the generations. Just the labels had changed. We explained to

Mum that it was a Shamanistic ceremony to effectively welcome Amelie's Spirit into this world. We said there would be drumming and singing bowls. Mum's love of music and history, her strong sense of curiosity, and a healthy skepticism were now convinced this would be something worth attending. She had seen something Shamanistic on the television, and she was up for a new experience, albeit with a little trepidation. Of course she loved the ceremony and especially the drums, which she really connected with. She surprised herself, as she was often apt to do. She especially loved the homemade cake, bringing the whole thing back down to earth.

Amelie was born on 10th August 2010 and Mum instantly fell in love with her. Mum loved the head of a baby, something about their shape and size, and Mum thought Amelie's was just perfect. She got to play in the Grannies' Cup in the autumn of 2010 for the first and sadly the last time. Over the following six months Mum watched Amelie grow and develop. We had the occasional coffee together, something we had not done previously, and it was fun sharing our discoveries with Mum (as any first time parent will know). Mum just smiled sometimes, as if to say, 'yes, you will learn'. Sometimes she was curious about how current thinking had changed. Mostly, she just watched Amelie. Mum was enchanted by Amelie's sense of curiosity. Rarely would Amelie sleep when we were out. Her eyes were constantly taking in whatever was happening around her. Alert should have been her middle name! She was a good sleeper as a baby and a good feeder and Mum's comments were: 'She is a good baby, she will be fine, she is a good eater and so alert. She is going to cause you a few problems as she grows up.' Then she would laugh and I would know that she was thinking... a little bit... about pay back. Mum never tired of my talking about Amelie's developmental changes over the months. I know she had been there before on several occasions, but never before had I been able to share my own real experiences with her.

Spiritual-Logic Insights

To engage with our Spiritual-Logic is to truly accept that different perspectives are as valid as yours – not more and not less. If we all thought the same way, reacted the same way, did the same things the same way, then life would be very limiting! In fact we would not survive if this were the case, let alone thrive. Yet, at our deepest level we are all the same – this is a human dichotomy! Celebrate the differences you see in the world – don't just tolerate them (that isn't good enough), because it is our differences that enable us to survive, support each other, thrive and evolve. We can do this within the security of knowing that underneath it all we are all the same.

We may have expectations of what we would like to happen in our life and we can call these goals or dreams. They may or may not materialise for us, especially if they involve the actions of other people. There are never any guarantees and this we must accept or we are destined for disappointment. When we define exactly how those expectations should be met, we also deny the possibility of progress. There are many routes to the same destination and not everyone will take our route.

Developing Spiritual-Logic

- ✓ Be wise. Don't allow yourself to be threatened by different perspectives. Instead approach the situation with curiosity and a desire to learn.
- ✓ Stop arguing. Every perspective is correct given the information that the person is working with in that moment. With new information we can all change our perspective.
- ✓ Approach the challenges you face with softness and a desire to understand rather than aggression and feeling threatened.
- ✓ Do not judge or be critical of others. We are all imperfect and we are all the same. Our human logic just doesn't allow us to see ourself that well!
- ✓ Take full advantage of the opportunities that come your way, because you don't know how long they will keep coming.

Life is Changing – December 2010

The weather leading into the winter had been cold and we had already seen snow. There were forecasts of more snow and mum had not been able to get out and play golf since the Grannies' Cup. Mum enjoyed seeing the snow but always wanted it gone as quickly as it came, mainly because it restricted her movement. She wouldn't drive in the snow, which was probably a sensible decision. One less driver on the roads is a good thing in snowy conditions, even if they are competent. On the brighter snowy days she would still take her much-loved dog Monty out for a long walk. Monty was named after Colin Montgomery, the famous Scottish golfer. He was famous at that time for being the most successful golfer never to achieve a Major. Mum adored both her dog Monty and the golfer. Monty was a Highland Terrier, on the rather stocky side of healthy and he was always to be found not too far from Mum's feet. Mum reasoned that the way to keep him chilled out and happy was to ensure he was well fed. She applied the same principles to her family too!

Mum loved the feeling of crisp snow under her boots and the dog loved it too. They would wander slowly and carefully down the road and into the fields and back again. They were both happy to walk at the same pace. Monty had long given up trying to run around like puppy and had easily adapted to the sedentary lifestyle. He also grew very protective of Mum, so it was never really very clear who was looking after whom.

Mum used to comment how the snow has a cleansing feeling about it. Not only because it is the purest white you can ever imagine, but also when it falls it has a shine so bright it can only give you a feeling of purity, like a fresh cut diamond. It brightens up even the darkest horizon, especially when seen from the warmth of your front room. Mum's house looked out over fields and the snow stretched out over them like a warm blanket, snug tight yet resting ever so lightly on the ground. How could you not love the snow from this perspective? More snow arrived, and more after that too!

On 11th December, Murielle and I became civil partners. It was something that we had talked about before bringing a child into the world, and now Amelie was four months old. We were both a bit anti-commitment and the idea of becoming civil partners filled us both with some level of anxiety. But we agreed that committing to bringing up a child together in our relationship was about as big as it gets, so a civil partnership would simply formalise that commitment and also help with the process of my adoption of Amelie.

We broke the news to our mothers that we were going to become civil partners, which they were delighted about. Then we told them that we were going to have a quiet ceremony with just the two witnesses. They were both devastated and in no uncertain terms told us so. I knew deep down that Mum would probably not take that kindly to us going it alone, but I did not expect such a strong reaction. Naïve maybe! Stuck in our own heads… probably! We had lots of good reasons why we wanted to do it alone, as I am sure most people do, but there was no way Mum was going to let that happen. Mum proceeded to tell me that it was a part of Amelie's history and therefore it should be done in a way that would give her something to remind her in the future that she is part of a bigger family unit. Mum was adamant that she wanted to be there. Murielle's mum reacted the same way, desperate to be there and support us as we made this commitment together. We couldn't have got it more wrong if we had tried. Now, Murielle and I both being fairly strong-minded women could have easily made our point by sticking to our guns, but something, perhaps intuitively, told us this wasn't an appropriate battle to fight.

Some things happen that cause you to seriously re-think your thinking and re-think your connection with people and with life and this was one of those times. Really, what were we thinking of, to leave out the most important people of our own lives just because we didn't want to make a big deal of it? We were denying them the experience of supporting us in what they both considered (as do we) a serious commitment to one another. They so deeply wanted to share this sacred event with us and we just wanted to blow it under the carpet! Our mums were of course absolutely right. All arguments I could present to myself about: wanting a quiet event, not wanting to be the centre of attention, not wanting to spend money on it, that it was a paperwork exercise because the real commitment was already undertaken with Amelie, that they wouldn't mind because… all of our arguments had no substance and we really were missing the point!

We are all connected and the sharing of experiences, for good or bad, is what unites us.

It is the sharing of experiences that adds to the richness of our lives, it leads us to grow and develop and to become who we really are. Our positive memories are what keep us going when life gets tough. They give us hope for a better world or a better future and they remind us that our life was a good one and worth living. Given what was to follow a few months later I have never been more grateful to whatever force of nature (or force of Mums) that had us reconsider and create a small, private, intimate and wonderful day that was enjoyed by our family and some of our closest friends. Mum had her favourite roast rib of beef and it was excellently cooked. She talked for ages about what a gentle and lovely ceremony it had been. She really loved that day, as did we. We made absolutely the right decision… in the end… and thanks to both our mums for their insistence.

It is a truism that you cannot please all the people all of the time, and to try to do so would be in vain – because to feel pleased is a choice we individually make. To compromise your desires/actions for another is generally considered an admirable thing to do and often expected as the norm within relationships. This, though, is human logic. If we do not consider that our compromises are our choice the inevitable consequence is to feel someone owes us something or that we are being under-valued. Then, at some point in the future, we will seek payback or revenge in order that justice is served. When we do not make our compromises a choice, we will hold it against the other person. If we feel that we choose to compromise, we do not actually compromise at all, and we are then able to support others with a truly open heart!

Christmas was upon us again. It is strange how it seems to come around more and more quickly as the years go by. Whilst in the Army I had always managed to get back for Christmas Day and volunteered to work over the New Year. The New Year celebrations weren't something that inspired me, but Christmas was something very special – it was family time. In my late teens and early 20s, after Mum and Dad had gone their separate ways, we spent several Christmases at Mum's brother's house. They had a bigger house than us, more money and loved a lavish Christmas celebration. Booze was free-flowing and there was more than plenty of food. Being young at that time and still living with the idea that extravagance was a good thing, it was the ultimate in opulence by middle-class standards and it was great! There were presents galore, packed under the Christmas tree and along the wall of the living room, literally hundreds of them. There would be anything between 11 and 15 people attending over a period of three to five days in all. It was a big family gathering and much louder and excitable than normal daily life. Mum loved those party days too. I think on the back of her divorce and free to do as she pleased, it was a great opportunity to reconnect with her side of the family and share in fun and laughter. A form of therapy in its own right. And boy did we have some laughs.

Apart from those big family Christmases, presents were never much of a feature of our Christmas celebrations. It was always about the idea of quality time as a family, sharing food (of course) and just being together. Often we would set a budget of £10 per person in order to make the challenge of buying significant gifts more interesting. Over those years our family situation was of course changing, the younger children were now young men and women. Several of the key people at those earlier Christmases had now passed away. There were no grandchildren and the nature of Christmas gatherings was different. I started to spend Christmas Day with my partner at the time, and so our family Christmas Day shifted to Boxing Day.

The fact that there were no grandchildren in our family, especially that Mum had four children, none of whom had produced grandchildren, was a heavy burden for her to bear. She used to reminisce about Christmas with more than a hint of sadness, especially after her own mother passed away in 1995. The Christmas fairy tale of happiness and childlike fascination is something that, if we are lucky, we get to experience as children and it remains with us. We may even try to recreate it year after year, because it felt so good back then. Mum struggled with the changing times, struggled as most people do to recreate that wonder and awe of a child's Christmas experience. But, because she was who she was she found new ways to entertain herself and Boxing Day really did become our Christmas Day... albeit different. We stopped getting quite as drunk and instead talked philosophically about life and our experiences, we still played silly games, because that's part of the fun, and of course we still had more food than we could eat.

S-L

Unfulfilled expectations, and especially those that involve others acting in a particular way, will always lead to disappointment. Expectations are of human logic and lead to us 'fixating' things in our mind – to see them as consistent with our own thoughts. This is antagonistic to change and therefore limiting. Change is an inevitable consequence of time passing and this idea of change must be brought into our minds and hearts for us to be able to accept things as they now are. Wishing, with sadness, for things to be as they were, will always result in us experiencing a struggle to 'let go', and therefore prolonging our suffering. Keeping those traditions that serve us well is an act of respect.

Letting go is not about releasing the love we have, it is about releasing our desire for permanence. When we let go we can maintain our love without pain.

This Christmas Mum made her traditional Christmas trifle. It was the only time of year that we ate trifle so we made the most of it. Not one, but two huge raspberry trifles. They were gorgeously soft, tasted great and were terribly filling, but we had to eat at least one large portion each and of course with loads of double cream! The second trifle was given to Murielle and I to take home. Mum always made enough food for each of us to take stuff away with us. It was all part of the Christmas spirit. Trifle, Christmas pudding, booze, Christmas cake, and every year there was boiled ham. Boiled ham was probably Mum's favourite Christmas meal – eaten for breakfast. In the past we would have it with a Bucks Fizz (champagne mixed with orange juice), which would mean we were gently half-cut by lunchtime. Over the years we had dropped the Bucks Fizz so we could see the day out, but the ham and pickles with crispy bread were still a must-have and what wasn't eaten on Christmas morning hit the buffet table on Boxing Day, or in our case hit many tables on Boxing Day as it was shared among the family.

By now Murielle and I had already agreed to alternate our Christmases, spending one in Brighton with Murielle's family and then the next with my Mum. We thought this would be a fair way to go and everyone would know in advance what our plans were. Because this year Amelie was only four months old her first Christmas wasn't going to be a massively exciting affair. She didn't even know what Christmas was and had no expectations of it. So we agreed to do Murielle's parents this year and we would go to Mum's for Christmas Day 2012. Mum was okay with this plan. She had long since become used to me not being there for Christmas so this wasn't anything new to her. Nat spent Christmas with Mum and they had a lovely day together. I still rang her several times on the day to share what we were doing and find out what she had been up to, as was the norm for us.

We had a family gathering at our house during the week between Christmas and New Year and Mum came to that along with both my sisters, their respective partners and our closest cousin, who was actually a cousin by marriage but one of the hard-core family members of the 'good old' Christmas days. We had a buffet-style menu as is often the case for post-Christmas events as we get to use the leftovers that way. There were eight of us in total, so not a large group by past standards. It was a cold day. Mum was picked up because she had become a bit more anxious about driving and this meant that she could feel more relaxed. If she had to drive she would be limited to daylight hours, and she would have been on edge the whole time, staying for about an hour before going home, to be sure she was back before dark. She was getting to the stage where she felt she wasn't able to negotiate the journey, even though it was simple enough and she had driven it a few times before. We had noticed her becoming more reluctant to drive over the previous weeks and had put it down to the wintry weather conditions. As time progressed though, Mum's lack of confidence in driving became a significant indicator of a bigger problem.

Mum arrived and she let it be known that she wasn't happy, as she was a bit sharp with her remarks right from the start. She could be quite forthright and didn't suffer fools gladly, so it wasn't anything new to us when she was a bit feisty, but with the benefit of hindsight, she was a little sharper and feistier than normal. Mum was never great in groups, even in family groups, and the older she got the harder it was for her to enjoy being herself in larger groups. In a one-to-one situation she was a completely different person. When in a group, she would sometimes react in a way that seemed out of character and she could easily end up either shocking or offending you. I didn't ever believe it was her intention to shock or offend, she just wasn't comfortable and didn't really know how to express herself without it coming out like a complaint or a dig in some way. This day was one of those days, but where she would normally respond to a comment like 'settle petal', today she didn't. In spite of the fact that she was with her closest family she was overly critical of everything. The food was late, the house was cold, she couldn't get warm, no one was listening to her and she wanted to go home almost as soon as she arrived. We were all used to mum, so we ignored her musings and carried on… eating and chatting. As the year drew to a close, little did we know what was to come in the following months.

Change doesn't care what we like or don't like – it happens anyway!

Spiritual-Logic Insights

To engage with our Spiritual-Logic is to value change rather than fear the consequences of it. Whether we like it or not matters not, in so far as change doesn't care what we like or don't like! Change is a major aspect of our human existence! Our resistance to change can result in great misery, for us and for others. This is especially relevant when we resist the ageing process because this represents so much to us in the context of our mortality. The reality that we are getting older may be one of the hardest things for our ego to take. Accepting and going with the flow of change is key to our experience of inner peace. Anything less than acceptance and flow is to long for something that cannot be and such longing is the cause of sadness, distress, illness and suffering.

The recognition of our parents' ageing can be a challenge for us, because of the expectations we have of them which have, for the most part, arisen from our childhood concept of them as mum and dad. As children we don't expect our parents to age, to be wrong, to be ill or to die (unless of course they are sick when we are a child – then it is all we know of them). If your parents have been strong-willed, determined, feisty, competent, caring, loving, then at some level of your human logic you expect that to continue, perhaps into eternity.

Waking up to the reality of what is happening enables us to support each other more effectively.

Developing Spiritual-Logic

- ✓ Do things for others without the expectation that they will return the favour… and if they do something for you, give gratitude and receive with love.
- ✓ When you feel resistant to anything that is pushing your boundaries, take a deep breath, pause, tell yourself all will be fine and then go with the flow.
- ✓ Know yourself, know others and allow both the time and space to change. Just because you think a particular way today, doesn't mean you have to be thinking the same way tomorrow.
- ✓ Flexibility is not about being indecisive or a doormat! Make decisions because they enable you to appreciate how powerful you really are (when your energy is focused) and to learn about the ingredients that create the outcomes you want, and then be prepared to change anything if it is appropriate to do so. This is the art of being flexible.
- ✓ Allow the past to be what it was. Show gratitude for it having got you to where you are now. Then, only take into the future the things that support you now. Allow others to do the same, and take into their future all that they choose!

Damned Arthritis – January 2011

Mum always started to think about golf in January. Even though she rarely started playing properly until about March/April, her feet would be getting itchy and she would turn her mind to getting her golf swing going again. The winter was on its way out and we were heading towards the spring. There was a sense of optimism in the air as she could see the end of the dark nights and mornings. On days when the weather was good Mum would venture to the end of her garden and begin her swing practice. For a long time she had a golf net at the top of the garden and she loved to practise throughout the year. The previous year she had removed the net because it was rotting. She didn't replace it. Instead she hit her oldest balls straight into the field at the back of her garden. She never hit that many balls at any one time now, literally no more than half a dozen. That was usually enough for her to feel she could maintain her swing. She reckoned that the two prize pigs that inhabited the field wouldn't notice and that the balls would be buried in the mud within a day or so!

We had spent many an hour together hitting balls into that net. We had a great deal of fun putting it up too! It was the perfect place for any consultations regarding her swing and we didn't have to go too far to pick up the balls! On many occasions I would be summoned to have a look at Mum's swing. There were key dates in the year for this: February, because it was the pre-season preparation; April, because Mum needed to recover her swing from playing golf when the ground was still quite wet; and then sometimes just before she played in a major event. Mum's swing never took very long to fix – most often she would only have started to speed up and try to over-hit the ball. She would have been trying to get distance on her shots, but instead she always resulted in losing distance and control of the ball! Getting her swing back into rhythm was all it took for her to get into her stride and feel that she had her control of her game again. Mum was always grateful for the tips I gave her, yet she would argue bitterly at times that what I was saying was too simple and there must be something else going on. Once she realised it was that simple she was the happiest golfer in the land and ready to take on anyone. She loved talking about her golf and sharing the details of her rounds. I loved helping her and boosting her confidence. It was a win-win and something that I was grateful to have been able to give to her.

S-L

Sharing time (and being present with that time) is the greatest gift we can give, because it is of our self that we give. Money, possessions, our ideas and thoughts are of course things that can do a great deal of good in the world, but our own time is the most precious thing we have, therefore the quality of this gift to another is immeasurable.

Something that always impeded Mum's swing was her hands and this was particularly the case during the winter months and early into the golf season. Mum suffered with arthritis in her hands, which meant she experienced a great deal of swelling and pain making it difficult for her to grip the golf club. She sometimes had a problem in the late autumn, but mostly she was bothered with this condition around February. It had been getting a bit worse over the past three years or so, and with the snow the last couple of years, it had become more noticeable. But as the spring came and the weather dried up a bit Mum's hands recovered enough for her to get into her golf, although she would still be susceptible to bouts of swelling and pain throughout the year.

Now, it was January and this year Mum was already complaining about the arthritis in her hands. She was even more irritated by this than normal, perhaps because she was already irritated by the weather, but most likely it was because what she was actually experiencing was slightly different from normal and at some level she was aware that things weren't quite right.

Although we weren't aware at the time, Mum was getting pains in her head. She later said that they weren't really headaches. Mum was particularly aware of her head having suffered with migraines and sinusitis for at least 20 years, on and off. She knew what headaches were about and she knew what head and face pain were like, but what she was experiencing now was a different kind of pressure, so she knew it wasn't migraine or sinusitis she was experiencing. She really thought it was arthritis causing the problem in her joints – including her neck. One of the challenging things with Mum was that she didn't tell us everything that was going on, so we never got the full picture. I received some bits or even the same bits over and over again, but never the full picture. This is of course perfectly normal human behaviour, because we give our attention to the problem we are experiencing in the present often in isolation, and we forget! We are not always trying to put together a bigger picture – just working with the symptoms we are experiencing right now. Even the medical profession works a bit this way in their diagnostic process.

Unfortunately though, if you don't get the full picture it also makes diagnosis difficult. Mum was herself a problem solver so she had already worked out that this was all about her hands and neck and arthritis. Of course, this is an appropriate conclusion when you have pins and needles in your hands and a pain in your head. It could very well come from a trapped nerve and tension. Mum was doing the human thing – working with the information she knew about and she wasn't able to see beyond that. Sadly, Mum's self-diagnosis was a contributing factor in the way in which she was treated by the GPs involved and indeed to the way in which her family responded to her.

In order to 'see' we must learn to look beyond our own interpretation of how things are. We all operate within the limited framework of our conditioning and it may take someone outside of that to help us to 'see' clearly. It is in this respect that consulting like-minded people, or agreeing for the purpose of appeasing, do not help us.

Our sense of independence, demonstrated through our desire to problem-solve something on our own, can get in the way of us sharing the raw data of our experiences with another person. If we can make things stack up logically, we can also fail to see because in our mind we already have the answer.

There was a way to go yet until spring as we had another good couple of weeks of snow. It came down really heavily over a few days and hung around in the cold air. Mum's early optimism was chased away after the first week of snow. She was beginning to feel trapped again, because getting out of the house was really quite treacherous. The snow became compacted and was very slippery. Even walking up and down her 200ft back garden was becoming a challenge. Monty would get dreadfully wet and end up with sticky snowballs all over his chest, which Mum would then have to clean off him. She was finding it all hard work and she was becoming more irritable because her hands were causing her considerable pain. Day-after-day in a small two-up, two-down cottage, for someone previously highly mobile and active, was starting to feel a little soul destroying. At least that was how Mum described it. She was also feeling lonely as she was unable to get out and see her neighbours. Mum would eat more, exercise less and become generally fed up in those early days of the year, but this year seemed just that bit worse than previous years. Her optimism for the offerings of spring were stifled by the reality of the cold and icy weather that was keeping her trapped in her house.

Mum would call me several times a week and January was traditionally a difficult month for conversation. I never knew whether she would be in her optimistic state and wanting to talk about getting back into her golf, or whether she would be irritated by the lack of mobility. Mostly this year it was about the snow, feeling trapped and being very irritable. It was becoming wearing already and it was only January! Of course, we were all living our lives and consumed by our own troubles and stresses. Murielle and I had a five-month-old, we were exhausted, work was challenging because I was feeling out of alignment and in the throws of re-positioning myself, and we were in the process of opening new offices, with all that entails, in an economic climate that was heading into depression! So, having to deal with regular calls from an irritated and frustrated Mum at this time was particularly challenging. My stress levels were rising and my tolerance was diminishing by the day. Roll on spring and the better weather!

Spiritual-Logic Insights

Engaging with our Spiritual-Logic is to become aware of the natural limited nature of our human functioning. Even though we know a great deal about a lot of things in life – through science and research – there is still a great deal more that we do not know. Our knowledge is bounded by our own world and to think what we cumulatively know (let alone what we individually know) is anything other than the tip of the iceberg is one of the biggest illusions we can live by, and can only result in feelings of isolation and/or the illusion of power. Of course, we like to think that we know because it provides the illusion of security, which is important for us to feel safe. If we think that we don't know something we can either feel challenged because it throws us into a world of insecurity, or we can simply recognise that this is just the way things are, and in doing so realise our connection to a much bigger world of which we are unaware. The latter results in a feeling of connectedness and inclusion.

Our sense of 'knowing' something to be true fixates our perspective in respect to that thing – which simply means we cease to look for an alternative perspective which could explain what is going on. We mentally operate through simple cause and effect principles (A causes B), when in fact we, and our lives, operate through far more complex mechanisms than this. We operate like the frog. If you put a frog into warm water and heat the water it will kill the frog, because it doesn't notice the water getting hotter, but if you put it into hot water it will jump out immediately! We get used to our own physical, mental and emotional experiences – we also acclimatise very quickly to subtle changes such that we easily and quickly consider them to be the norm. We also see other people in the same way – which means we may not be alert to subtle changes – especially if they are just more of the same! When we really tune in to our intuitive self though, we stay awake to these changes and in doing so we may ask more questions.

Developing Spiritual-Logic

- ✓ Always give your time, even when you are feeling stressed. A smile can change a life. Sharing your joy can brighten the world. Saying hello can provide the feeling of safety and connection.
- ✓ Know that it is your human logic tendency to seek certainty and stability and to make the world fit to your model of the truth. Then go and seek uncertainty, instability and having your model of the truth shattered, so that you can stay awake to the subtle changes that are taking place.
- ✓ Be aware that our sense of 'independence' can blind us to the needs of others. Learn to receive from others and find out what others need.

- ✓ Accept that the more you know, the more you realise that you don't know and feel liberated by this fact – it shows you how vast the world is.
- ✓ Don't feel threatened by your own feelings of insignificance. You may never truly know the impact you have made in your life. Trust, without the need for evidence, you are more than you think you are.

The Delusion of Hope – February 2011

February came around and we had two birthdays. Mum was 72 on 3rd February and Murielle was 37 on 6th February. We usually tried to do something for Mum's birthday. Either we would get together as a family or have her over for lunch, or sometimes we would go out for lunch. On this occasion we didn't arrange a lunch, but I took Amelie around to see Mum on her birthday. She wasn't feeling too well. She was feeling very tired and her hands were really irritating her. She was struggling with Amelie who was being quite demanding, so it was a quick visit. Nonetheless Mum loved seeing Amelie who was already, at six months, keen to be on her feet. Amelie always made Mum smile, with her facial expressions and newly developing mannerisms. Mum loved children, and was particularly fascinated by the shape of their heads and she loved the shape of Amelie's head. As she watched Amelie you could see the connection she had with her. Mum's love for her shone through, even though she wasn't feeling great. Mum was feeling a bit anxious about Jakk's wedding as she was going to be giving her away, which meant she had to give a speech to the guests, and she wanted to feel better for that. She hadn't been feeling that well for a while, with the arthritis in her hands, and things didn't seem as if they were lifting, but it was early in the year yet and the weather was still damp.

S-L

Hope has great power because it can lift us out of challenging (but not life-threatening) situations, but it can also blind us to what is really going on. Hope enables us to live with the illusion that things will improve.

We had Jakk's hen do on 5th February. She was getting married on 5th March and Nat had arranged a wonderful do, making chocolates and having a gorgeous meal at the Malmaison Brasserie in Oxford. We met at Jakk's house. Mum was lively and looking forward to the day ahead. None of us had made chocolates before. Some of the guests were on the champagne as we arrived at Jakk's house about 11am. I was driving Mum in my car and the other girls were going in a minibus because they were planning a late night of it. Mum and I were coming back after the meal. She was proud to see her daughter preparing to be married and that had the grandchildren bells ringing for sure. Little did we know, that Jakk was actually already pregnant. Maybe on some unconscious level mum knew, but she didn't say anything until Jakk's wedding in March.

Mum's behaviour was already changing. During the chocolate making she made some strange comments and then at one point started throwing chocolates at the other girls. Although this was done in fun, for Mum it was completely out of character to behave in this way, with her family. I sat opposite

Mum during the chocolate making and was completely thrown by her behaviour and told her so. At the time I was aware of how strange this was for her, but made some 'sense' of it because I knew she didn't like being in bigger groups. Who knows what I put it down to: just Mum being Mum; Mum being stressed about the forthcoming wedding; Mum not quite herself. The point is that I knew things with her were starting to feel out of sorts, but what she was doing was still within her normal range of possible behaviours (just a little out of context at times). It was all so subtle it was impossible for me to really realise what was happening in front of my eyes. Maybe, I was not 'seeing' beyond my human logic.

The day after Jakk's hen do mum was really exhausted. It was as if she had put every ounce of energy she had into the day and it really did knock her sideways. Her hands were still playing up and if anything getting worse, and for the first time she told me that she was dropping things. She complained of tingling sensations in her fingers and not being able to feel things properly. She also mentioned that she was struggling to put her bra on. What she didn't say was that she was struggling to remember how to put her bra on, which is a different level of problem! And I didn't ask the question either! A few days later she called me. She was stuck in bed and had been sick... in the bed. She didn't feel able to move to clear up. She was feeling rough. I called Murielle to come and look after Amelie and rushed over to her house and she did look poorly. She thought it might have been something she had eaten. We both agreed that she had really been through the wars this winter, what with one thing and another. I changed her bedding and asked her if she wanted me to call the GP to come and see her. She said she would give it a couple of hours and see how she felt. Mum was never one to inconvenience anyone and that included the medical profession. She would always say they were busy enough with really sick people! I stayed with her for a while, made her some toast and a cup of tea. She started to feel a bit better.

S-L

With hindsight it is easy to see the pattern of deterioration developing, but in the moment we are so engrossed in our joint history, our conditioned relationship to each other, that we don't 'see' clearly. Accepting this is part of our human condition is essential. If we don't accept this fact, then we will tend towards feeling guilty for not acting sooner – and guilt is one of the most destructive emotions we can hold on to.

Over the following days Mum said she was feeling increasingly exhausted. She visited her GP surgery on several occasions in February, sometimes twice in the same week, complaining about her hands, feeling tired and generally unwell. She was diagnosed with hypertension, which is basically stress. Her upcoming daughter's wedding was thought to be the main cause of Mum's anxiety. She was certainly anxious, that was becoming very clear by the day. At times she was visibly shaking. She was reluctant to go outside her house and she was very anxious about driving because her hands were not functioning properly. But, with hindsight, the scale of anxiety was beyond even Mum's scope for pre-wedding nerves. She still called me regularly, almost always complaining and frankly driving me up the wall. As far as I was concerned Mum had been diagnosed with stress and therefore she had to learn to relax, be more physically active, do the postural exercises she had been recommended by the doctor, and stop worrying about things. She had to start to change her thought patterns to change how she felt. The doctor had said so. She was offered the opportunity to see a psychologist to help her with the stress, but she said she would speak to me if she needed that sort of thing. Mum also said she didn't feel that stressed, something that none of us really took on board at the time.

On one level I know I was very aware that Mum wasn't well and things didn't seem to be improving. Yet I was also caught up in our personal history and my desires for her to improve. Mum had historically on occasions deferred to the 'woe is me' approach (as we all do) to get attention and especially at this time of year… it being the back end of a long winter, with her feelings of loneliness and frustration with inactivity. She called me a lot at this time of year to help boost her morale. Only this year I had my own family, with a young baby, which was taking my energy and attention, and I didn't have the emotional energy to take Mum's problems on board.

Mum was a big worrier. She would share her worries and concerns and I really took them seriously. Whether she did worry as much as she seemed to or whether she just felt better having shared her worries I never really knew, but she certainly evoked a negative response in me when she talked incessantly about things worrying her without doing anything about them! Mum had used me as her problem-solver and motivator, which meant she would tell me her troubles and expect an answer that pepped her up. Only now I didn't have any answers. I didn't know what was going on. I was as frustrated as she was and I didn't deal with her very well at times. Compassion hadn't yet registered in me and instead I was reacting through my own increasingly challenging life situation. It was a time of projection and counter-projection and probably the worst time in all the months that followed. It was a time when Mum's condition was getting worse, a time of uncertainty, and a time of no answers. It was not a good combination.

S-L

Giving people what they actually need – what they are crying out for – in the moment, may be more important than giving them what we think they need to improve or change for the future. There is nothing wrong with needing comfort, support, kindness, or needing to feel needed. These are not weaknesses, they are a part of our human condition. When we reject these things we deny our connection to compassion and love. Sometimes it isn't about solving the problem it's about being present to it.

Mum also started to grow more attached to her next-door neighbour, also called Helen, in a way that was uncharacteristic for her. She seemed to be developing a sort of idolized dependency, probably, in all seriousness because this neighbour was showing Mum a great deal of compassion and support, which was something that she needed and wasn't getting from me or her other children at that time. Helen is an exceptionally compassionate woman and was always wonderful with Mum. I was thankful that Helen was there, and for the amount of time and support she gave Mum throughout the course of her illness. Mum started to lean on Helen more and more, to the point that Helen was also getting concerned. Mum was starting to expect Helen to be there for everything and it was becoming a relationship that was not sustainable. I talked to Helen about it and we both agreed that what was happening didn't seem normal for Mum. It was one of the earliest and most obvious indicators that there was something significantly different going on. I said to Helen I was beginning to suspect Mum was in the later stages of dementia, all the symptoms were indicating that was a possibility. But the GP had diagnosed stress, so that was that. Until Jakk's wedding was out of the way and the perceived stressor removed we couldn't really see beyond that.

To put things into context, Mum was brought up in an era where doctors assumed the position of God, or at least pretty close to God. This means two things: firstly they know what they are doing (and are right), and secondly you do what they say. The GP recommended Mum to be as active as possible, learn to worry less and relax and that things would improve as the weather changed. I was in support of this increase in activity and getting out of the house. It is well understood that these things help overcome anxiety. So, we went out and around town together one day to get a few bits of shopping. Bless mum. We staggered around town. Well, actually that is a gross exaggeration. We made it very slowly from the car park to Marks & Spencer where we made some effort to look at a few clothes before going to their coffee shop. Sitting there I looked across at Mum and realised that she was dying before my very eyes. She said that she felt a bit better for getting out, but as I watched her drink her coffee she had an uncontrollable shake in her hands again. I know stress and anxiety can cause physical shaking but this was not the Mum that I knew just a few months ago. It was as if she had aged 20 years since Christmas and I was facing a 90-year-old now, not a 72-year-old. She was trying so hard to be positive and do what the doctor had said. The next day she was exhausted again.

I was brought up to respect doctors the same way Mum had. I knew they weren't God, but I had still given them more 'professional respect' (seen them as being right just because of the professional position they hold) than I should have. I had accepted their diagnosis even though my intuition was telling me that there was a different problem going on with Mum.

Intuition is that feeling we get that tells us something doesn't stack up or feel right. It's a sense of knowing that may not come from our human logical processing.

I know there was part of me that wanted to believe Mum was suffering with stress – and of course she was! Stress as a diagnosis rather than just a symptom would be the easy thing to accept and it meant that she could do something to help herself and change the situation. But as time went on... slowly... the diagnostic picture wasn't stacking up.

Mum certainly was stressed, that was obvious, but whether that was the cause of her problem or a symptom, was becoming increasingly unclear. Mum was becoming very moody, aggressive at times and put the phone down on me on several occasions when she didn't get the answer she was looking for. I was getting increasingly frustrated with her calls, which were beginning to always end badly. I was increasingly frustrated that Mum wasn't getting any better, because this was stress and therefore something she had some control over changing. I was frustrated with myself for not being able to help her and I was still having to deal with my own life.

Spiritual-Logic Insights

To engage with our Spiritual-Logic is to appreciate the need for and importance of compassion – for ourself and others. When we feel threatened by our own sense of inadequacy we will always respond without compassion. We stop listening, we stop asking questions, we stop 'seeing' and we act with our own best interests at heart rather than the interests of others – this is partly a function of our survival instinct and stress creates this response in us. To be able to offer heartfelt compassion we must first manage our own internal environment – including our stress. Then we can really see another's suffering and support them effectively.

We must live with a trust that others are doing the best they can – and we must balance this with a recognition that we are all working through an internal 'system', which includes our human logic, and within external 'systems', which are the rules, procedures and processes (such as medical diagnostics, governments and businesses) that we follow and live within. We need to see these systems for what they are – then we will ask appropriate questions and challenge what we are told for the purpose of understanding rather than just to criticise.

To idolize another human being (because of their status, knowledge or capabilities) is to consider them to be something more than they are and this can lead to unhealthy dependency or an abdication of personal responsibility.

Valuing and respecting another person does not require us to idolize them. It requires that we appreciate them for their contribution to our world without the expectation that they are perfect or can 'save us' and without the sense that they are 'more than' oneself.

Learning to trust one's intuition is the art of tuning into oneself in order to 'see' through the fog of our mind's making.

Developing Spiritual-Logic

- ✓ Hope – but do not be blinded by it. Realism is not being negative. Optimism brightens the spirits. Have hope for a peaceful death and be optimistic for the new future presenting itself.
- ✓ Tune in to your intuitive self by acknowledging any conflicting thoughts and feelings that you have. Suspend your logical self in that moment and go with your intuition.
- ✓ Take what you see seriously in the first instant, rather than dismissing it as the normal way of things. When you expect things of others because they are specialists in their field, accept that they are also capable of human and even technical fallibility, so if you feel all is not right ask, find out, challenge, but not for the purpose of power play, simply because you desire a solution.

- ✓ Always communicate through the energy of compassion, which means to firstly recognise the suffering of others (rather than feeling threatened by them or what they say). Give compassion in what you do and say. Feel compassion in your heart, in order that you may approach life through the energy of love rather than fear.

- ✓ Use hindsight to change the future rather than blame yourself for being inadequate in the moment!

'Seeing' the Blindingly Obvious – March 2011

The week before Jakk's wedding Mum had shown a few signs of improvement in her energy levels, but she was so concerned with her hands not working properly that she booked a private appointment with a neurological specialist. As soon as she told her GP she had done this they also booked her in for a neck scan. On the surface the GP's actions were entirely appropriate for the symptoms Mum went to them with. Tingling in your fingers could easily be the result of a trapped nerve in your neck, so a neck scan is the obvious choice of action. Mum's appointment with the specialist was booked for the 8th March, three days after Jakk's wedding.

We picked Mum up to make the journey down to Maunsel House for Jakk's wedding on Friday 4th March. The weather was clear although still a bit chilly. Mum was doing her best to look forward to the wedding, but really struggling with her own health. She was exhausted, feeling anxious and her movement was slow and deliberate. Mum, Murielle, Amelie and I were staying in one of the guest houses belonging to the estate, which was a short walk from the main house. We arrived in the afternoon and had a look around the main house. It was gorgeous, stately, authentically medieval. Mum and I both agreed it wouldn't be our cup of tea, but it was just perfect for Jakk and Mike. A medieval theme throughout, one could imagine a number of ghosts frequenting this stately home.

S-L

To truly understand another's perspective is to fully appreciate their choices, without judgment or criticism. It is the doing of this that creates the feeling of being acknowledged and listened to, which are essential ingredients for our development of Spirit and Self.

We checked into our guesthouse on the estate. It had a subtle medieval ambience about it. We were greeted in the hallway by a stuffed fox and a series of rather gruesome looking hunting implements, which set the scene for the rest of the house! The bedrooms were on the ground floor and the sitting room and kitchen were upstairs. It was the first time that we came to really appreciate the level of Mum's deterioration. She was completely disoriented by the fact that the downstairs was upstairs and vice versa. Worse than that, when she moved around she was actually, literally, bouncing off of the walls. She couldn't walk in a straight line on her own. Now it was clear that this was a serious health problem. I know that stress can do strange things to people, it really can upset one's normal functioning, but this was definitely more like a significant and immediate onset of dementia – at its worst level. Mum's balance was all over the place and we were all now very worried. She was very confused. In spite of the fact that we were in a new place, this was not my mum! My fears that she really was dying were being strongly reinforced by the scale of her symptoms and the speed of her deterioration and I felt helpless to do anything about it.

Mum struggled her way through Jakk's wedding. She was giving Jakk away and although Jakk had to virtually carry Mum down the aisle to keep her from falling over, she did manage to thank everyone for coming. In all honesty, Mum couldn't have done any more if she had tried. She gave everything she had in her tank. Problem was, her tank was running on a negative balance.

The wedding was a beautiful affair. Jakk looked gorgeous, if a little drained, and Mike had a grin across his face as if he was the cat that got the cream. Mum, in one of her lucid moments during the proceedings looked at me and said, 'she's pregnant'. In that moment Mum had a real twinkle in her eye, but it was soon gone, replaced by a dull sadness that told me she was really not well at all. 'Mum' was gone again, replaced by the symptoms of extreme dementia.

The next morning she was feeling a bit better. Her mood had lifted and she was positively reminiscing about the wedding and how gorgeous it all was. She was such a proud mum. She also seemed a little more oriented and less confused. Maybe it was stress after all! Ever hopeful of a simple solution, I know it was something I wanted to believe. Mum certainly seemed a lot happier after the wedding than she was before it.

S-L

Each of us has a level of physical and mental tolerance to stress (which also affects the functioning of our physical, mental and emotional self), beyond which we become ill. There are those who say that we need some level of stress to function effectively at all. There are many stressors we have to navigate in this life – the obvious ones such as addictive substances, external factors, food toxins, and then the less obvious ones, such as our physiological and genetic predisposition, our thoughts, feelings and attitudes and of course, unidentified diseases. The removal of a stressor in our life will always have a positive impact on our ability to function and can give the illusion of an improvement. To say where or what the balance of stress is for any human being may be a bit like playing God and none of us is that evolved!

We got back from Jakk's wedding and Mum went to see the specialist. She told him about the tingling in her hands and that she was concerned about driving. She said she didn't feel safe because her hands weren't working properly. She wasn't as tired as she had been and therefore didn't mention it. She also didn't mention the fact that she was confused and disoriented and worse still, neither did I. In all honesty I didn't think to because I was under the impression the doctor would do a thorough neurological check and would find anything that was wrong – without my input. He checked Mum over, focusing on the symptoms in her hands and said that he thought she was actually getting better, given how she said she had been prior to the wedding. Now this was what we both wanted to hear. That was brilliant news we both agreed. He was working of course with the tingling in her hands and did all the relevant neurological tests for those symptoms. He never looked into her eyes, which, I came to understand post-diagnosis of the tumour, would have been very revealing at that time. Mum and I went away feeling a little brighter, because she had been given the 'all clear' by a specialist, but she was still not feeling confident that she could drive.

Over the next couple of weeks Mum's symptoms didn't actually get any better. She was noticeably losing the ability to use her left arm and hand, unless she gave it a great deal of thought. She also started to feel sick on occasions and said that she felt it was a struggle to swallow. She was still feeling very tired. Everything was effortful, including the most basic tasks such as dressing herself. One of the challenges for us was that her symptoms would come and go. They were never a constant feature and the symptoms varied. Mum would say that she had struggled to put her coat on. Watching her, it seemed as if she wasn't concentrating and she wasn't aware of the left half of her body at all. Yet at the same time, it was also so subtle that at one level it didn't appear that serious.

I was concerned that Mum didn't appear to be getting any better and, having checked on the Internet, I thought she had late onset dementia. Little did I know that the symptoms for the brain tumour she was subsequently diagnosed with are virtually the same. I accompanied Mum to an appointment with her GP on a couple of occasions. At this point they were still talking about stress. I said to the GP that I was concerned Mum had late dementia symptoms and that there was a noticeable change in her character, but nothing was done about it. It is difficult for doctor's to diagnose a brain tumour for several reasons. The symptoms vary and if a patient reports different symptoms at different visits to different doctors the chances of them putting the pieces together are slim. I had bought into the stress diagnosis too. It seemed to make sense at some level and of course I wanted that to be true. But, as the weeks went on, it became clear this was not just about stress. I was getting increasingly frustrated at a lack of responsiveness from the GPs and I was looking for an opportunity to get Mum into hospital where she could be properly assessed. On the morning of 20th March that opportunity came along.

S-L

When you cannot create an opportunity yourself, perhaps because you lack certain resources (whether those resources are time, money, knowledge, power, confidence or some other type of physical or mental resource), you have to be awake to 'see' the opportunity presented to you, then take it with both hands. The act of being 'awake' brings those resources to you.

It was Saturday 19th March and Mum was feeling so poorly that she called the GP to her house. Her blood pressure was through the roof. She was exhausted and feeling pressure in the right side of her head, around her ear. Her mobility was severely affected and she was unable to balance or move unassisted. The GP came and went. The next day Mum was still unwell and in pain around her right ear. I was in Brighton at Murielle's parents for the weekend. I called Jakk and asked her to take Mum to the emergency doctor. She did this. Mum was diagnosed with a middle ear infection and sent home. Ironically, the appointment was at the local hospital where she was to return a few hours later. Jakk called me as soon as she had taken Mum home. She said, 'They have said Mum has a middle ear infection, but I think she is having a stroke. I think I have just seen her face droop.' I told her to call an ambulance and get Mum into hospital.

This was the opportunity we needed. They would have to scan Mum's head now and we would be able to find out what was going on. Even a stroke was beginning to make more sense than stress. Murielle and I had seen these stroke symptoms in Mum a couple of days earlier, although we hadn't mentioned it to each other at the time. Within two seconds her face drooped and then recovered itself. What I didn't realise at the time was that minor stroke symptoms (TIAs, or Transient Ischaemic Attacks) happen just like that. When I saw it I wasn't quite sure if I had seen it or not. It happened so fleetingly and Mum was back to normal within a flash. I wrongly assumed that stroke symptoms wouldn't just disappear like that. With it happening again it had to be something significant and related, and in any event it was the opportunity we needed to get Mum's head properly assessed.

S-L

Ignorance is a part of the human condition. Sometimes that ignorance is down to a lack of knowledge, which is inevitable on the basis that we cannot know everything. The most challenging aspect of ignorance though is our ignorance of ourself. We fail to see all that we are and all that we can be. We don't want to look because we cannot cope with the reality of how fallible we really are and yet we never look for our beauty and power. We live our life through illusion and delusion (delusion is thinking our illusions are real!), hiding from ourselves and seeking the solution to our problems from the outside world. Waking up to ourself is to free ourself from the illusions that we live by, so that we can truly live.

Jakk took Mum to hospital and thankfully she was admitted and immediately given an MRI scan. Mum was taken to the stroke ward and we were called in to see the stroke specialist on Monday 21st March. Jakk had to be in work that day, but my brother, Malc, Nat and I went to the hospital. Mum was already on steroids, which could only mean one thing. There was something going on in her brain. As we stood in his office I could feel the pain. I knew deep down what I was about to hear. I think truth be told, we all knew. The good news he said was that Mum hadn't had a stroke, but unfortunately there was a problem – she had a brain tumour. It was quite significant in size, located on the right side parietal lobe above her ear, hence the symptoms in her left side. He was so factual! The specialist was a wonderful man, so gentle and kind. He was also very clear that this was not a recoverable situation. It was without doubt malignant and the treatment programme would have to be decided by his colleagues at the John Radcliffe Hospital. He never built up our hopes or expectations in any way, nor did he limit Mum's options by what he was saying – he was very matter of fact with compassion.

As we approached Mum's bedside our faces must have painted the picture. She was as much herself as she could be. 'Right, give it to me,' she said with a determined voice. 'What's the score? Don't hide anything from me, I want it straight.' She could see by our faces that the news wasn't good, but even she wasn't expecting what was to come. 'Mrs Emms, you know you had an MRI scan yesterday and we have given you some steroids to help you now… we thought you might have had a stroke, but I am pleased to say you haven't had a stroke. But, unfortunately, you have a tumour just above your ear on the right side of your brain.'

As I heard his words I also felt my heart aching as it was breaking. I knew I had to be strong for Mum and my sister, and I also knew my mum had in some respects already gone.

She was not the person she used to be, parts of her had already died before now – I had witnessed that over the last few months.

The specialist proceeded to explain in simple terms that Mum would need to go to the John Radcliffe in Oxford for further treatment and that they would decide what needed to happen. Until that time she would stay comfortably where she was and take the steroids, which would help with her symptoms. The steroids certainly did that. Within a day Mum's mobility in her left arm and hand was much improved... deceptively so, as it would have been easy for us to raise our expectations seeing such improvements. Mum did at last look more relaxed than I had seen her in what felt like a long time. For good or bad she at least had an answer to the problem she had been carrying around for the previous two months. She felt listened to and safe!

S-L

There is a great deal of talk about the 'law of attraction' and that we attract our experiences to us – including our illnesses. This, whether true or not, is a particularly harsh concept to propose to someone who has not been brought up with an appreciation of the impact of their thoughts and feelings on their health. One might even question whether the Law of Attraction is simply a human logic concept born out of our inherent desire to have full control over our world! No one can say categorically that we cause our own illness through our thoughts, emotions, behaviours and attitudes. The range of factors that must come together for any event to happen – let alone illness – is significant in number and complex in nature. We know this to be true because not all people who smoke die from lung cancer and not everyone who drinks excessive alcohol dies because of liver failure. Both of course will be contributing factors to our death, but it is almost impossible to say what the 'specific cause' is – because to do so would be to narrow down the world to simple black and white 'A causes B' responses.

I will never forget the expression on Mum's face as the specialist was talking her through her situation. I could hardly bear to look at her, as it was taking all my strength to do my best to hold it together. I was in shock, yet not surprised in the slightest. I had seen this, yet not wanted to believe it. Maybe at some level I had been in denial – but in my mind I simply hadn't believed it because I didn't have the hard evidence – and I had hope. Now it was very, very real, clear and undeniable. Mum was dying. It was now just a matter of time. How long exactly, I didn't know. I intuitively knew she wouldn't see Christmas, I just hoped she would see Amelie's first birthday and the birth of her second grandchild.

Mum was her typical pragmatic self on the outside, yet I could feel her pain on the inside. Her pain was as clear to me as if I had been given the news myself. I wanted to take it all away from her. I wished it was me sat there, not Mum! I also realised that wouldn't be fair to Mum. It would be harder to see her daughter dying than it was for her to be the one leaving. After all, this is the natural order of things. Mum went into 'processing mode', as was her way: planning, making sense, wishing, hoping, believing, not believing, strategising, theorising and more. She said she wanted to go into a hospice, then the next minute she wanted to go home. She was clearly in shock... who wouldn't be. Even to this day, I cannot imagine what it feels like to be given this news. At one level there must be an element of relief – even if that is only because you have an answer.

Death is an end to everything we know in this world, including the pain, the sorrow, the hardship and the stress. It is inevitable. But it is also the end of the love, the happiness, the fun and the hopes and wishes. It really is our ultimate eternity and when you are given notice for it that must be a strange thing to deal with. Well, over the coming months we were going to do just that. We were going to deal with whatever was thrown at us... together, as a family and to the best of our abilities. Mum just turned to me and said, 'Well that explains a lot doesn't it?' I said, 'yes Mum, it explains everything.' There was some comfort in that moment, comfort in the fact that at last we had an explanation and Mum wasn't going mad!

I left the hospital following the diagnosis, which in and of itself was a hard thing to do... to leave Mum alone with her thoughts when all I wanted to do was to take it all away from her. I got in my car and screamed the word 'no' for what seemed like forever. 'No, no, no.' I cried, more than I have ever cried in my lifetime and I couldn't seem to stop crying. Nothing was going to stop the flood of tears. My heart had literally been ripped apart – I could feel the exact spot in my chest where this was taking place. I was experiencing the absolute realisation that a huge part of my life was coming to an end. That special baby, born on 3rd February 1939, who became my mother, was not going to see the one thing she had wished for since giving birth to her own children: her grandchildren growing up. This caused me the greatest sadness and I was very literally feeling gutted and heartbroken.

S-L

Our emotional experiences provide the richness in our lives, as the colours, smells and textures are the qualities that make the natural world what it is. It is through our emotional experiences that we remember, and we develop our stories – the stories that remain with us and that we share with others. When we embrace our emotions in the moment, let them flow and then let them go, we live life fully. Avoiding and holding on are symptoms of our human logic and can never lead to inner peace and contentment.

'Special' is a human logic label. Such labels are used to categorise things within our world. To do so is to differentiate one thing from another. To label something as special we

create the potential for feeling a greater sense of loss if that thing is taken from us. Spiritual-Logic is about enjoying the 'specialness' we give to something without the sense of loss – we can only achieve this when we accept that we own nothing and that everything we do have will leave us (or us it) eventually.

Mum spent a week at the local hospital whilst they were stabilising her condition with the steroids and waiting for a bed at the John Radcliffe. She met some very wonderful nurses and physiotherapy staff. She was particularly taken by the two male physiotherapists who were excellent with her. One came from Liverpool with a strong Scouse accent that entertained her no end. She loved those boys and I think they were quite fond of her too. In fact when she went back to the same hospital later in the year they both came to say hello.

The physiotherapists would come round and do a daily assessment, checking out Mum's range of mobility and functioning. She would chat them up one moment and then put them in their place when they were late for her appointment, in the next. It was all very light-hearted and Mum was enjoying feeling looked after and comfortable. She felt safe and was getting back to her cheeky self. It was fascinating to watch them at work and appreciate how they were putting together the pieces in order to work out what help Mum would need in the future at home. It was fantastic for Mum because it gave her something to strive to achieve.

It gave her a sense of independence, which was important, and something positive that she could work towards for the future. She really could see that what they were doing with her was going to help her. Her faith was being restored and most importantly she was feeling listened to at last. She had been right, she had known there was something wrong, but she hadn't imagined a brain tumour. I am not sure if she thought her progress was a sign that she could beat the tumour or not. In all honesty, it didn't really matter, it raised her spirits and that was something for her to live for at that moment in time. Mum's attitude of fascination in the process she was now going through was to remain with her over the coming months.

Mum was transferred to the John Radcliffe in Oxford and after several more scans and consultant discussions they decided that they would undertake a biopsy, which meant removing a small sample of the tumour in order to ascertain the most appropriate treatment plan. The location of the tumour made removal impossible, since to do so would have, at the very best, rendered Mum completely paralysed down her left side. These decisions are never easy and the quality of life of the patient is now a clear priority in the process. The consultant was speaking directly to Mum about her condition and the procedures she was to undertake, which also meant that the messages we got from her weren't always the reality of what was happening. Whether that was because she simply misunderstood or forgot or she just wanted to protect us from any bad news we will never know, but I suspect there was certainly an element of wanting to protect us all. Suffice it to say we were working with messages that were often confused and even contradictory. It was clear that confusion and contradiction would be one of those things we were going to have to learn to deal with over the coming months as Mum's condition progressed.

Mum was beginning to acknowledge that she had cancer. She had made the connection that her brain tumour was in fact cancer. She had known plenty of people with cancer and the end result was never a good one. Her brother's wife, Jo, had died a few years previously with a brain tumour and there were seven people at her golf club, all of whom had been diagnosed with one form of cancer or another in the period November through January. Mum was fascinated as to how so many people could be diagnosed in such a short space of time. She used to say 'what on earth is going on with us all?' Mum reflected on Jo's situation and this caused her to feel really quite down. She was aligning herself with the same outcome, which was also the reality. We stressed how different Mum's case was: Jo's brain tumour was a secondary cancer whereas Mum's was primary, which made a difference. So then she reflected on another lady at her golf club who had recently had brain surgery of a different kind. She was up and about around the golf club now, although still not playing 18 holes – this gave Mum something optimistic to grab hold of and a sense that there could be a future, if only for a short number of years.

S-L

It has been demonstrated that when doctors give patients a timescale in respect of the prognosis for their condition, that very often they live to that very point in time. This is aligned with the fact that what we believe to be true we can make true for ourself. But, it is also the case that timescales have come about as a result of doctors observing the patient's progression through a terminal illness. There is no doubt that our beliefs (together with the beliefs of others) are very powerful in shaping our destiny, but belief alone is not the panacea for curing illness and to think that we can is an illusion of human logic. Yes, we do have an impact on our destiny as a function of our beliefs and thinking because clearly any decisions we make are based on these mental processes. Yes, we can impact the experience of our symptoms through our beliefs and focus of attention. But, belief alone cannot prevent death when the organic functioning of the body is so dysfunctional – if it could there would be many people who wouldn't have died who have and our doctors really aren't that stupid! If belief alone could cure a terminal illness they would be prescribing it! Spontaneous healing involves something in addition to the patient's belief – something that lies beyond our beliefs in the realm of faith and Spirit and it operates at the deepest level of our Soul. And, more importantly, healing does not always mean 'to cure', it can also mean to 'wake up' – to heal ourself of our limited thinking and inhibitions that hold us back from achieving our highest potential in this life, rather than to prevent death.

I have no doubt that Mum knew she was going to die because on one of my visits to the hospital she looked at me and said 'I am not ready to die, I wasn't expecting this.' Those words will stay with me forever and are probably the saddest words I could ever hear her say. But, it was the reality for her at that time. Mum was really still a young woman, active and with so much to live for. She had a young grandchild and another one on the way, she loved her golf and her garden. She definitely wasn't ready to die. The fact that she was contemplating this told me she knew that death was the ultimate outcome of her condition. What she didn't know was how long that process would take and no one gave her any indication either. In her mind I think she thought she had a couple of years and she was planning for that. My view was to let her plan for whatever she wanted, the process of the disease would take its course and we would face the changing reality as and when it happened. So that's the approach I took with Mum over the months that followed.

Mum's surgery took place on 28th March. They had been able to take more of the tumour away than originally planned. They call this process a bulk removal. It is definitely better than a biopsy because it removes some of the impact of the tumour immediately. Mum was over the moon. She was planning the things she would do when she got home, and all was well with the world. Now she definitely had years to play with. The steroids were already showing their affects and she was on a high dose, so her cheeks had puffed up, but her mobility was almost back to normal. She was also struggling with sleep at night, and hallucinating, which are apparently common side effects with steroids. Mum was extremely confused but pleased that progress was being made. It was challenging for us to know exactly what was accurate and what was Mum's imagination playing tricks on her. It would have been very easy to ride the illusion that we desired, which was that Mum's future would be changed as a result of the process she was going through, but the reality wasn't going to change and that had to be accepted. She was very proud of her scar though, which was an L-shape down the side of her head and then across the top of her ear. She went into great detail as to how the operation was carried out: that they pulled the flap back and then had to laser through the three holes she now had in her skull. She talked with total fascination and admiration for the skill and technology that had made this all possible. GPs might not have been God any more, but her surgeon had definitely been assigned godlike status.

One of the many benefits of being at the John Radcliffe was that the food was fantastic. Mum had been warned of this while at her local hospital so she was full of expectation for an exceptional dining experience. Her expectations were fully realised. The food there was exceptional, which was a good thing because when on steroids your appetite goes through the roof. Mum was permanently starving. We took in loads of food parcels of biscuits and sweets and all the naughty things you could imagine. She consumed the lot between the meals that were provided and was still hungry. Mum's permanent state of starvation was to be the source of much humour and entertainment over the following months and she wasn't the only one who gained weight as a result!

Spiritual-Logic Insights

To engage with our Spiritual-Logic is to be open to the infinite possibilities that are available to us without closing down the route we feel we must take in order to achieve them. It is not for us, as human beings, to play God by saying what is right or not right for another person, and especially if, in doing so, we limit their options. Therefore, any actions we take or thoughts we share, should as far as is possible, increase or enhance their options and add value to their life. Even then, this is best achieved with their permission rather than without it.

When supporting someone with a terminal illness it is important to tune in to them, where they are at – which will change as time and their condition progresses. In order to achieve this, one has to suspend one's own issues, desires and fears. Enabling another to feel empowered rather than disempowered is the greatest support we can give. To empower another person is not about problem-solving for them so much as it is about being present with them and acknowledging their experience, so that they feel listened to, cared for and involved.

When our experience of fear is strong, it is possible for us to tune out completely – as if to protect ourself from things that we don't want to know about, because we don't know how to handle it. We stop listening; we disconnect and effectively withdraw – as if frozen. Recognising how resourceful we actually are and having faith that no matter what happens we will cope – even with death – builds self-esteem and Spirit.

Developing Spiritual-Logic

- ✓ Listen, listen, listen. And I mean really listen. Not to what you think you have heard or to what you want to hear. Listen not just to the words someone is saying, but tune in to their emotional voice. Acknowledge their deepest experience in the moment.
- ✓ Always seek to understand rather than change or problem-solve. Ask questions to get the full picture, before coming to any conclusions, theories or solutions.
- ✓ When you know the details, don't be constrained by them. They are a guide and not definitive in any way, unless you make them so in your mind. Keep open to alternative possibilities rather than settling for the one that you want to hear!
- ✓ Learn to manage your own stress so that you do not project your 'stuff' onto others. Mood swings are not 'normal' so see them as a sign that something is not the way it should be.

✓ Take care of your words. Say what you are going to say in your head first and then ask yourself whether what you intend to say is going to limit or enhance the other person's options. Speak with purpose and volition, rather than just for the sake of filling the silence!

Buying Time – April 2011

Mum was in the John Radcliffe for a week before returning to her local hospital pending her return home. The brain surgery had been a huge success, she had recovered well and she was now past the post-surgery danger period, which is the time when she would have been most susceptible to fitting. Once back at her local hospital she started working with the physio boys again. They were making sure she could use the kettle and work appropriately with her left arm and hand, which meant that she had to really think about what she was doing. Our brains are very clever and if one bit isn't working properly other bits take over. We become used to this new way of doing things (which is called accommodation) and then we struggle to relearn how to do things properly. Mum had accommodated to the weakness in her left arm and was automatically doing things with her right arm that she would normally use her left arm for. Relearning was effortful and mentally tiring, especially following brain surgery. Mum was fascinated to learn about why she was doing things the way she was. She always asked lots of questions of the physio boys and worked hard to follow their instructions.

'It's all such a learning curve,' she would say as she opened the kitchen cupboard door with her left hand and then put her right hand into the cupboard to get the tea bags out. She had accommodated to doing the whole thing with her right hand – which is actually not the normal way of doing things. This simple process that we take for granted would take Mum three minutes to complete because of the level of thought that it required. Everyday tasks had become a mammoth challenge and although this had been building up over the last couple of months, starting with the putting on of her bra, it felt as if it had come to a head overnight. It was at this point we started to really discover the significant difficulties mum had been experiencing at home – some of those things she hadn't mentioned, others she had complained about and we simply hadn't given them enough attention.

S-L

In the hard, macho, western world we live in we are led to believe that needing another's positive reinforcement is indicative of a flaw in our make-up. As social animals if we deny ourselves such social connection we will die – both in spirit and physically. The level of reinforcement any one person needs will vary and will also change under different circumstances, such as when ill. We need to be awake to the level of reinforcement we need in any one moment in time. Having the positive reinforcement of others may go a long way to creating the quality of faith and spirit required for spontaneous healing to take place.

Mum was amazing. She took everything in her stride, with humour and dignity, and saw every task as a challenge. She delighted herself with even the smallest progress, constantly looking for that positive reinforcement from others. She was doing brilliantly and we continually reinforced this without building up any false hopes that she could beat the cancer. Rightly or wrongly, I was always clear with her that this was something she couldn't beat, but it was something she could have some control over. I always said to her, 'no one can tell you how long you have, so that bit is up to you.' I knew we weren't talking years. I had read up about what it meant to have a Glioblastoma Multiforme (GBM) Grade 4.

Now, I know there are many books out there stating that we have the ability to heal ourselves spontaneously – I have read many of them and I agree that we have the potential to heal ourselves. What I don't agree with is that healing necessarily means recovery or cure from an illness. Healing to me has a much broader application than curing an illness and in fact buying into the idea that we can cure ourselves can do more harm than good. When we think we can cure ourselves it causes us to raise our expectations of our own capabilities and then leaves us feeling a complete failure when we don't heal ourselves in the way we think we should. I have worked with many clients who have fallen foul of this human logic error of thinking. I am sure I could write a book on the subject, and maybe one day I will, but for now, where Mum was at, the healing she was going to do was going to happen through acceptance and being present. Anything less than that would be delusional. How long? That would be up to Mum and her God.

How do we live when we know we are dying?

Mum left hospital and went home. She was delighted. I am sure there must have been times over the previous few weeks when she thought she would never go home. We had moved the single bed down into the living room and set the room up beautifully. She was overwhelmed as she walked into her house. It was clean and tidy, just as she liked it, and everything was set up for her to live as normal a life as she possibly could. Living as normal a life as possible became our joint objective. Having spent some 20+ years in the field of personal development and for a long time been a subscriber to the idea of being in the present moment, never was this concept made more clear to me than now.

How do we live when we know we are dying? As I pondered this question I became even more acutely aware of exactly how much time we spend reminiscing our past and how fantastic things used to be (or reminiscing the problems of our past and wondering how we can escape them) and striving for a better future, because we don't like our current situation. When there is no future, how do you live as normal a life as possible? You practise the art of being present. It was now my task to help Mum to be as present as possible, making every day as special and normal as I could, almost as if a future did exist but we were so loving the current moment that the future didn't matter. Every day was to be an experience and strangely enough that's pretty much the mindset that Mum adopted too.

S-L

Being fully present in the moment leads to the feeling of deep inner peace and contentment. When we become totally absorbed in what we are doing, without comparative thought or judgment, without wishing or hoping – just 'being with', time stands still and we feel totally connected to our sense of oneness.

The next stage in the process was radiotherapy. Mum had been referred to the Churchill Hospital, which works alongside the John Radcliffe Hospital in the provision of a wide range of treatment programmes for cancer patients. We had a meeting with the oncologist who explained the treatment options available to Mum. Just before Mum left the John Radcliffe we had a meeting with the specialist Macmillan nurse on the ward who had already talked through some of the treatment options that are available. She had mentioned that radiotherapy was the most likely treatment given Mum's condition. She said there was a short-term treatment plan and a longer treatment plan. The short treatment plan takes place over three weeks and you have to attend twice a week, a total of six sessions in all. The longer treatment plan takes place over three months. The real effectiveness of the treatment plan is not fully appreciated until a period of time after the treatment, that is three times the length of the treatment plan itself. Although this sounds complicated what it meant was it would be a further three months following the short treatment plan before we would have any idea of the effectiveness of the treatment. The nurse said that the specialist oncologist would decide the most appropriate treatment plan for Mum. The nurse also mentioned that chemotherapy is a possible treatment option following a course of radiotherapy, but again that would be a decision for the specialist. Mum asked a few questions, enough to be reassured that something would be happening next. I think that while she could believe that some form of treatment was possible, it gave her hope. Hope for what I am not sure, possibly the hope of more time, but maybe just the illusion of hope is enough.

Our meeting with the specialist was brief. She showed Mum a picture of the scan of her tumour. Mum and I were both fascinated by the scan. I was also horrified at the size of the tumour. Mum fortunately didn't realise the full extent of the size of it. It is difficult enough to make sense of a 3D image being moved on a 2D surface, let alone when you have a tumour, you are 72 years old and not used to looking at a computer screen. Mum was in fact quite reassured by the image she saw because she had thought that the tumour spanned her whole head. It was cancer after all. Mum's idea of cancer, as is many people's is that it is all consuming. So she had created an all-consuming image of it in her mind. To see the lump only on one side gave her a great sense of relief at that moment. An interesting learning point for me at this time was the very real fact that there is a case for 'ignorance is bliss'! This was the time and place for it.

The specialist recommended the shorter course of treatment. Their main consideration is the quality of life that the patient will have rather than quantity – and rightly so. As a result of Mum's age, the type of tumour and its location, the shorter course of treatment was recommended. Mum was delighted. She saw this as a really good indicator that the tumour wasn't that bad. After all, if it had been really bad they would have recommended a longer course of treatment, was Mum's thinking. 'Yes mum, they have recommended exactly what is right for you,' was all I could think to say. My appreciation of the rationale for their decision was very different from Mum's. In the past, I would have shared my interpretation with her when we had a difference of understanding, but now was neither the time nor the place. 'Yes Mum' was becoming one of my most common responses to her interpretation of events, except on the odd occasion when she talked about beating the cancer. Being honest on that front was one of the most difficult things I have done – it would have been so easy to go along with her – and I am sure some people would be critical of my stance on this, but I knew it was what she would have wanted from me. 'Tell me straight' were Mum's words and while I wasn't about to tell her the exact details of what was to come, and I was prepared to go with Mum's thinking most of the time, I knew she would not want me to deliberately deceive her with some illusion of getting better, when her body was telling her something very different.

Mum chatted all the way home from the appointment about how lucky she was to be doing the short course of treatment. She didn't have a start date yet, but she was looking forward to getting going. 'What an interesting learning curve we are on,' she said. I said, 'yes Mum, it will be interesting.' When we got home, which was an hour's drive, she was exhausted and starving. 'How about fish and chips?' I said. I knew it was one of her favourite meals. We have a local shop that does great fish and chips, and although in the past it had been a rare treat, over the course of her treatments it became a more popular choice of meal. 'What a great idea,' she said. 'I will have a large cod and chips, and make sure you are having some too.' 'Yes mum,' I said as I jumped back into the car and drove into town to pick up the fish and chips. Having a few moments alone was necessary to refresh my thoughts, gather myself and re-group. I wouldn't have had anyone else take her to the hospital and I wanted to be with her as much as possible at every stage, but that level of emotional and mental input is challenging. Even 20 minutes in the car was a much-needed break, with half of it spent sobbing and the other half sorting myself out. The fish and chips were great, but I couldn't eat it all. Mum polished hers off and then asked for pudding! Eating became her favourite occupation and one she was very good at.

Spiritual-Logic Insights

Engaging with our Spiritual-Logic is learning to embrace uncertainty because it helps us to go with the flow of life.

Deluding ourself and others may seem like the right thing to do to prevent the experience of pain and suffering. But, in doing so we then also deny the potential of experiencing the power of acceptance – with which comes a sense of inner peace and calm.

It is our relationship to 'time' that impacts our ability to be in the present moment. If we feel there is never enough time we cannot get our mind to be still. When there is 'no time' (in the sense of no future), the mind can be still and we become present with what is happening now. When we see our experiences for what they are and suspend our judgment of them as either good or bad, desired or not, we can remain present – with no desire to change that moment, just to engage with it – for what it brings to us. This is more easily achieved if we have faith that our experiences are intended for our higher purpose – even if we cannot see that purpose. This is why there is 'no time like the present'.

Developing the quality of patience enables us to 'give time'. If we are in a rush there is never enough time to give and we feel that time is constantly being taken from us – the result of which leads to our experience of irritation and frustration and even that time is passing us by. Time will pass. It has to. It is our concept of time, rather than the ticking of the clock, that we can control. Patience enhances the qualities of calm and peace and also helps us to develop a sense of mental clarity.

Developing Spiritual-Logic

✓ Be fully with the person when you are with them. Don't allow your mind to wander for too long into a future without them, or sadness at the loss, but if you do stray, then share it with them. If they are still here you need to be too.

✓ Be patient. Whatever you are personally feeling, take a deep breath, look at the bigger picture and be patient. You (may) have time that a dying person does not have!

✓ Give positive reinforcement – praise, support, encouragement, compassion – when they need it. Don't defer to what you think might help them. Always acknowledge another's pain rather than trying to solve the situation for them.

✓ Change your relationship to time in order to develop patience. There is always enough time. Most of what we think needs to be done is of little significance or consequence when you really look at it. Get your priorities straight! If you were going to die in the near future, what would be important to you?

✓ Allow others to remain ignorant if it harms no one and helps them – but be sure to raise your awareness to wake up to your own ignorance in order that you can achieve your highest potential.

'It is all a Learning Curve' – May 2011

Mum's dates for treatment came through. The dates I couldn't do, Nat was able to do. Jakk and Malc were working full time. I was fortunate to be able to give my time to Mum and thankful for a very understanding partner who made that possible. Nat was also available and in fact moved in with Mum for a couple of months to support and care for her. The journey to and from the hospital took its toll on Mum. It was an hour each way and most of the route took us along winding and uneven roads. Mum felt every twist and turn and bump in her head and complained bitterly. 'I am sorry mum' was all I could say. 'I will do my best to avoid the bumps.' But the reality was that this was a standard road surface and nothing I could do would change that. Mum's head was very sensitive and she felt every movement – it caused her a great deal of distress and discomfort. She was aware of everything that caused a change in her head and mentioned that it felt like there was water moving around in there. It must have been very disconcerting. Fortunately, she wasn't in pain, as such, just destabilised by the inside of her head feeling as if it was moving around in a water tank. Who wouldn't be?

In the first instance Mum had elected to be picked up by the wonderful volunteer drivers who take people to and from hospital. It sounded like a great idea. Mum thought it would be nice to be with other people who were undergoing the same sort of treatment, a bit of a comforting and yet sociable event, but in this case it didn't work. The first appointment was a nightmare. Nat was with Mum. The driver was due in the morning and didn't show up. Now, one thing with Mum was that you could never be late. Timeliness was next to Godliness in her mind. She was a very timely person and always early for everything. Late was not an option, and if you were you suffered for it. Not only was the driver late, there was no indication of when he would show up. Understandably, in this particular instance Mum was very frustrated. The trouble was, when she got frustrated now it really wasn't fun to be around. She would become quite aggressive to whoever she was with, even if it was nothing to do with them and she would want solutions quickly, even if you couldn't provide them. Understandably, it caused her a great deal of stress and distress and this then resulted in further confusion and anxiety. In this case it was Nat who bore the brunt of it and her solution was to drive Mum for her treatment. From then on, either Nat or I took Mum to her appointments and we were never late again. That was one small hurdle crossed.

The first radiotherapy session Mum went to she had to get her mask fitted. This is a very precise procedure, whereby plastic netting is moulded to the shape of the face, which enables the head to be held in a specific position for the radiotherapy treatment. This was a fascinating experience and one that Mum often talked about afterwards. Mum absolutely loved her mask and the woman who fitted it for her was a wonderfully caring and compassionate soul. She was brilliantly talented and very kind hearted. Mum looked at her mask and said, 'my goodness, all these years I thought I had a big nose and look at this. It's tiny. I really have a tiny nose.' She was overjoyed with the fact that she had visible evidence that she had a tiny nose. Only mum could think that way! Mum continued to turn her experience of radiotherapy into something positive and uplifting every time she went to the hospital.

We soon got into the routine of the treatment journey and Mum came to accept that some trips would be good, others not so good. She approached the treatment as she had done the rest of this journey, with a sense of curiosity and fascination. On the second session Nat and I both went with Mum. It was indeed fascinating to see the huge radiotherapy machines. They are a bit like I imagine giant spaceships to be. As we walked into the room, which was otherwise quite sparse, this huge metal construction with a name on the front of it, a bit like the name given to the lottery ball machines, stood looming over a hard metal table. Nat and I stood by the door while the nursing staff helped Mum onto the table. Mum was manoeuvered into a specific position before they attached her mask to the table. This enables the beams of radiotherapy to specifically target the tumour in the places they have identified via the scans. This is done with complete precision and setting the head in the right position is the lengthy part of the procedure. As I was standing watching Mum being put into place it hit me again that she was dying, and my heart was ripped from me... again. I struggled to control myself and both Nat and I walked out rather swiftly. God bless Mum, she was chatting away with the staff and taking it all in her stride as if she was heading into a dressing room to try on clothes. What else could she do? I, on the other hand, was wrecked and so was Nat.

The session was over in a flash, literally. The actual treatment lasts only about seven minutes. Mum was being escorted out of the room before we knew it, still chatting away. She had just one complaint... she had only managed to play three holes of golf and was just about to sink a putt when she was interrupted. Fantastic. My heart lit up and all was right with the world again. All those years of practising visual imagery for her golf and here she was now, using that most amazing skill to keep herself entertained whilst a tumour in her brain that was killing her was being fried by radiotherapy beams. There is a lot I have still to learn about my mum, I thought to myself as we all walked towards the café.

S-L

Our ability to use our mind: to generate ideas, see the future, re-arrange the past and even go over and over our problems, requires us to wake up to the fact that we do have control over our mind rather than 'it' (our thoughts) happening to us. What we use our mind to focus on is a choice. It requires us to exercise desire and discipline: the desire to focus on something specifically and the discipline to stick with it. This practice is achieved through meditation and mental rehearsal. Without this skill our mind will wander, as minds do, and any sense of inner peace will remain just an idolized concept!

The café became one of our joyful rituals during Mum's treatment programme. However, to get to the coffee shop we had to go past a rather nice little clothes shop. Well, that was a bit like giving Mum a licence to print money. Mum was never extravagant, rarely shopped for herself and generally speaking hated clothes shopping. It was as if she was letting go of some repressed aspect of herself now. If she wanted it she was going to get it. And mostly she wanted it. I understand from others that this desire to spend money is quite common among people with this type of tumour. I was also told that it was something to do with the steroids, which may or may not be true. What I do know is that in some way she was trying to take control and build a future for herself. She was buying clothes that she, in her mind, would wear once she was through all of this. Of course, this idea now presents us with a challenge because this part of Mum that is preparing for a brighter future and a new her is not accepting the current situation at all. Mum spent hundreds of pounds at that shop over the six times we went to the hospital. She never wore any of the clothes she bought and we could have pretty much predicted that she was never going to wear them. Mum didn't really have that sort of money to spend either. But I for one wasn't going to try to stop her. From my perspective she was doing something that would give her a feeling of control in her life. It is important for all of us to feel in control and I can only imagine that when you know you are dying the last thing you feel is in control. If shopping gave Mum a feeling of being in control of her life and creating some sense of normality, then so be it. It was going to come to an end at some point and when it did we would pick up the pieces.

S-L

Nothing dampens the Spirit and crucifies the Soul more than feeling powerless – yet this feeling of powerlessness is of human logic design when it comes as a result of feeling you have no control. Letting go is the route through to the world beyond control – where life really happens. In this place Spirit cannot be touched and Soul is driving the bus!

We sat in the coffee shop. Mum was walking with sticks now. We had picked up some skiing sticks a few months earlier so that mum could wander out with the dog in the snow. Now they were coming in to use on a daily basis. Mum's movement was very slow and she struggled to breathe after just a few paces, so going anywhere was a real effort. You certainly couldn't be in a rush.

Mum got into her latte coffees at the hospital café. She needed to drink through a straw because she couldn't hold a cup stable enough to drink out of it and she was struggling on and off with her left arm and hand. Going for a coffee enabled us to take a break from the car journey and also give Mum a bit of time following her treatment. She said she felt fine. She often questioned whether they had actually done anything and we laughed about this a lot. We would sit and chat. We had officially been told that Jakk was pregnant and Mum would mull over how she never thought of Jakk as being the one who would have babies. She always saw Jakk as being a bit more independent and Nat as the one who was quite homely. 'How wrong you can be,' she said. She was delighted that Jakk was pregnant. One day we were sat in that café when Jakk sent a text of her 12-week scan through to me. I showed Mum and she was in awe. She said she could see the baby's head. I said, 'yes mum, isn't it wonderful.' The reality is that I couldn't make head nor tail of the very small black and white image on my phone, but if Mum could then that was fine with me.

One of the conversations we had in the café was about the use of visual imagery. Because I knew Mum was doing her own golfing imagery during her radiotherapy sessions I thought she might be interested in a theory about imagery helping with cancer. Often when people think of dealing with something like cancer they think of fighting it. Most people in that position would probably say that they were going to 'fight it'. Cancer, though, is an aggressive disease so meeting aggression with a fighting mentality can only result in resistance and quite literally a battle of wills. So I talked Mum through some research that had suggested it was better to give love to the cancer cells, through visualisation, rather than fighting it. Love always breaks down resistance, which may result in the cancer being less aggressive. Clearly you have nothing to lose and everything to gain. I said it wasn't going to cure it, but it might help slow it down.

Mum loved the idea. It made total sense to her. She was aware that the whole purpose of the radiotherapy was to slow the growth of the cancer down, so if this might help that process too then she was going to do it. Of course, practising these things is easier said than done, but Mum did it for a while and as a result became calmer and more accepting, but as time went on and with the tumour having a greater influence on her mental functioning any form of visualisation became more of a challenge.

> *Meeting aggression with a fighting mentality can only result in resistance and quite literally a battle of wills.*

Mum progressed her way through the treatment programme with courage, dignity and total respect for the staff who were helping her. Mum was always so polite to them, thanking them for their help and telling them how grateful she was that they did what they did. She told them all that they should be paid far more than they are. She certainly gave them her vote and she was absolutely genuine in her praise for them. That was fairly typical of Mum to see others as being worse off.

She was always one for the underdog and she never lost her sense of respect for the people supporting her over the coming months.

Some treatment days went better than others. Some days she was better able to cope, others were a lot harder. It was very much a journey of ups and downs. Mum never struggled with the over-tiredness that the specialist had predicted happens with radiotherapy. She only had a couple of days where she was absolutely wiped out. The rest of the time it was business as usual. In fact, she was still struggling to sleep as a result of the steroids, but the dose of steroids she was on couldn't be adjusted until the radiotherapy course had been completed. At that point in time the Iain Rennie nurses would begin the process of adjusting Mum's medication to get the right balance of steroid, to enable her to maintain her mobility and functioning for as long as possible.

S-L

Gratitude tames the ego. It directs our thoughts to appreciating what we have in life rather than looking for more or better. It is a quality that is related to humility and such qualities are the essence of our journey towards compassion.

Mum was starting to get out in her garden as the weather was improving a little. She was getting bigger because of the steroids of course, but she seemed to have responded very well to the radiotherapy, although it wouldn't be possible to tell until a couple of months down the line. Mum lost a bit of hair around the areas that the radiotherapy had targeted, which she expected and she was most proud of that. I think it verified the fact that she had actually received treatment, given she didn't feel anything at the time. One of our shopping trips at the hospital had taken us into the hat and wig shop. Mum had picked up a couple of hats that were really quite trendy and she thought nothing of showing them off to her neighbours as she walked slowly up and down her garden. She was making the absolute best out of what really was a rough deal.

Towards the end of the month things took a turn for the worst. Mum started to struggle with her movement and had serious pains in her stomach. She owned up to the fact that she hadn't emptied her bowels for days. I think the reality was that she probably hadn't emptied her bowels properly for weeks. Suffice it to say, she was now suffering… badly. Nat was living with her during the week and I would take over from her at the weekends. I turned up on this particular Friday afternoon to find Mum curled up in agony. Nat was at a loss as to what to do. The Iain Rennie nurses had administered several enemas with no effect. We called the GP. He attempted manual removal, which has to be one of the most undignified processes you can ever go through. That didn't work so he recommended that I take mum in to A&E. If we waited for an ambulance to pick her up it would be a couple of hours at least and even then there were no guarantees, so I said I would take Mum in myself. It was 10.30 at night.

We arrived at A&E and sat waiting, and waiting and waiting. Mum was in agony, but that didn't seem to mean very much to the staff. It wasn't even that busy, which I would have thought was unusual on a Friday night. Eventually, at 1 a.m., mum was seen by a doctor. They again tried and failed with the enema approach several times, at which time another specialist doctor was called. He suggested he could do a manual removal. Mum was in agony, frustrated at the things she had been through already, fearful of course at what was happening and furious that she would have to go through that undignified process once again. Given it hadn't worked before she didn't have any faith that it would work this time. The manual removal didn't work and eventually at 7 a.m. Mum was moved from the A&E bed to a ward. At least this was a more comfortable place to be. We had been up all night. I was exhausted, angry with myself for not feeling able to do anything to help Mum, and I was beginning to wonder if this was the beginning of the end. Mum was very, very confused and disorientated. It was a frightening time because she remained very confused and delirious for more than a week. She was placed on a more appropriate ward in the hospital and began to receive the right treatment to sort out the significant blockage.

S-L

Our perception of 'unfairness' is one of the toughest challenges for us to get to grips with. Steeped in our 'child energy' and therefore a conditioned response, we have a strong appreciation of what we consider is fair and what is not. My human logic says that it was definitely not fair for mum to have to wait all night in A&E (especially given her terminal condition) and undergo the undignified and predictably ineffective treatment she had to endure. But life, and the way the world works, just isn't fair. We can choose to do our bit to strive for fairness where there is a battle to be fought, and we must also learn to accept that unfair things happen and there isn't a great deal we can do about it.

Mum would tell us stories about what was happening on the ward. They were always conspiracy stories. I was seriously thinking that she had turned a really bad corner and I wasn't alone in that thought either. One day she said that the doctors from the John Radcliffe had travelled over from Oxford just to see her and they were appalled at the fact that she was still in hospital and at the way in which she had been treated. They were going to speak to someone about it and get it sorted. The 'main man' as she described the JR registrar was apparently not happy at all and heads were going to roll. Although these situations were funny at times, Mum was very, very convincing. It was a real challenge to work out whether what she was saying was actually true or not.

One day she said to me, 'they haven't changed my pain relief patch you know, not since I have been here.' I said, 'of course they will have changed it Mum, it's on your records when it needs changing and they have to follow what's on your records.' Mum's patch was to regulate her pain relief, so it was quite important that it was changed every three days. I then found out that she was absolutely right. They hadn't changed her patch and it was now five days since it was last changed! Not only was I beside myself that the patch hadn't been changed, I was also left wondering how it was that Mum had remained pain-free without the medication, and if she was pain-free why was she being medicated for pain in the first place? Lots of questions and not a lot of energy to ask them, just leave you wondering. Sometimes we assume professional people are doing the right thing, but this experience has reinforced the fact that it is always worth asking the question.

One morning I got a call from Mum, she was not happy. 'I heard you,' she said. 'What are you talking about Mum?' I said. She went on to tell me that she had heard me talking with the nurses in the corridor in the night and how despicable it was that I should do such a thing. I was gutted. It took a great deal of effort to persuade Mum that I was at home and had been all night and therefore how could I possibly do that? I said to her that she should know me well enough to know that I wouldn't do such a thing. It was hard not to react badly to the things that she said given the stress we were all under. What she said could be so hurtful and untrue and yet at some level in her mind she believed it to be true. Fortunately, these incidents were few in number and Mum forgot about them after a few days, but that doesn't help matters in the moment.

One of the funniest incidents during this time was when Mum talked about the clocks in her ward. It was a small ward of four people and there was a clock on the wall to Mum's right and a clock on the other wall to her left. She was aware of the fact that she was getting a bit confused at times, although she didn't realise the extent of her confusion. I saw the clocks on the wall and said to Mum, 'well that doesn't help you does it? Those clocks are telling a different time' (one was 2 p.m. and the other 8 a.m.), 'how do you know which is correct?' Mum looked at me as if I was completely stupid, then at the clocks and in all seriousness said 'that one is the time today and that one is the time tomorrow.' Well, I nearly wet myself. That was surely the funniest thing I had ever heard Mum say. The sad thing is that she actually believed it.

Eventually, some ten days later Mum left the hospital after what was most definitely the worst experience of her life. I think at times she questioned whether she would ever get out of hospital and this did nothing for her anxiety levels or her sanity. She just wanted to put the whole experience behind her. As she recovered, she did exactly that. In fact, after we left the hospital I don't think I heard her refer to it ever again. It was something that had happened along the way. The constipation was the result of the codeine medication that Mum had been taking since March. With her medication now changed, there wouldn't be a repeat of that situation. She came back to her house, which was also now fitted out with a hospital bed, commode and other items that would make her more comfortable, but were a significant indicator that things were changing. The Iain Rennie nurses brought round a bag of drugs for us to store upstairs, just in case Mum started fitting. We put them upstairs and we all moved on from the experiences of the month.

Spiritual-Logic Insights

Engaging with our Spiritual-Logic is to fully appreciate our experiences without making things personal. It is too easy for us to assume others are 'out to get us' and that they are saying things to deliberately harm or hurt us. But, when we do this we are simply failing to appreciate an aspect of the human condition – which is that we speak through our own pain.

Added to this, when someone is not of sound mind – by which I mean their mental capacity is deteriorating daily – to assume anything in respect of their intentions is to credit them with a greater level of control over their mental and emotional functioning than they actually have. The qualities of patience, compassion and acceptance enable us to ride the storm and continue to give the best of ourselves.

Do what you do with courage, receive what is given with gratitude and be present in order that you can make every moment the best experience it can possibly be.

Seeing the funny side of events is a great release and when in stressful situations enables us to put things into perspective. Childlike humour lightens our Spirit and softens tension. Sarcasm and cynicism are not forms of humour as they can easily be perceived as threatening or insulting, especially when you cannot guarantee how they are being received.

Developing Spiritual-Logic

✓ If you feel guilty that you should have done more – ask yourself, did you deliberately choose to not do more to punish the other person? If the answer is no, then your guilt is unwarranted and you need to cut yourself some slack for expecting too much of yourself! If you answered yes, you need to forgive yourself for the pain you feel in respect of the person you wished to punish. Neither of you are to blame. Then forgive that person for the mistakes they have made towards you, so that you do not feel the need to punish them again.

✓ Even in the darkest of situations allow yourself to see the funnier side, from a childlike perspective (which means less serious). Do not engage in sarcasm or cynicism or demean the situation in any way. Be humourous, but only with compassion and love.

✓ If you feel things are unfair, it is probably because they are! Recognise that life is unfair, that is not likely to change. If you feel something was not deserved, it is probably because it wasn't! But life doesn't run to our rules. Instead, accept that all things happen for a reason and sometimes it is best for us not to try to reason why.

✓ Let 'normality' be the way of things for as long as possible and know that time will sort out the details. Don't put your own life on hold if the person dying is benefiting from you sharing your life experiences with them.

✓ If you feel angry, learn to let go of that which angers you. Anger helps no one and just blinds you. It may be that you need to forgive. It may be that you need to stop trying to control and accept things as they are. These are not passive acts that leave you feeling a sense of hopelessness. They are empowering acts that enable you to operate at your highest level of human functioning.

Stopping Time to Live – June 2011

The summer was technically upon us even if the weather didn't entirely align with the month. We'd had a wonderful spring, warm and dry. June was okay but typically British: unpredictable, wetter and cooler than we would like. None of that really matters when you are dying though. Traditionally, we Brits have an obsession with the weather. It is one of the things we talk about a lot and mostly complain about. Mum had been no different and as a golfer had come to live her life by the weather. It didn't stop her playing golf, unless it was really bad, it simply dictated what she needed to wear. Now though Mum took joy out of the weather no matter what was happening outside. She was in fact taking joy from most things at the moment. She was feeling much brighter and seemed to be responding really well to the treatment. Whether one could go so far as to say she was experiencing some form of remission is impossible to say. She was at least feeling better than she had done since the treatment started and the chronic constipation that had interrupted life in the previous month.

Mum had decided on her return from hospital that she needed to make the front room a little different, because she was going to be living in this room now for quite some time.

Clearly, previously she must have had some idea that she might be able to move upstairs again at some point. She had mentioned the idea of moving upstairs early on, but we had always said that was not going to happen. Now she had accepted that would never happen and was planning to live in her living room, so she was going to furnish it just as she wanted it. She sent me out to get new bedding: quilt, covers, pillows and cases, sheets and bedspread and curtains. All were colour-coordinated in a soft green that matched her sofa. The armchair had been removed from her living room to get the hospital bed in place, but the sofa was still there. I went to the shops and came back with everything that Mum had asked for and we dressed her room. She was absolutely delighted. It was worth every penny to achieve that sense of comfort and joy for her. She did complain, of course, about the way I had put up the curtains, but that was to be expected. 'We'll have to get Helen in from next door,' she said. 'She knows how to do these things and you haven't got a clue.' 'That's a great idea,' I said, 'because this is not one of my strong points is it Mum?' 'No it's not.' We agreed. Mum was as happy as she could possibly be. She was content to remain here forever and if we could have frozen time during the course of this process, now would have been the right time to do it.

Mum's mobility was still quite good. She was walking with her sticks outside the house and moving slowly and carefully. She wandered up and down her garden, sometimes at a good pace compared to the recent past months. She was doing her damnedest to live a normal life, which included putting the washing out, cooking, and cleaning for herself. She was so proud of whatever small task she achieved. But, often her body didn't quite follow her mental instructions, so things like cooking were still causing some problems and she also got very frustrated with the simple tasks that she wasn't able to do.

Within a short space of time, things were slowly going wrong again in Mum's head. Some of the symptoms she had experienced before her diagnosis were re-appearing. She wouldn't remember how to fold certain items of washing, including a handkerchief. She had long since stopped trying to put a bra on, which was a significant source of distress, as Mum didn't like presenting herself without one. She also became quite demanding, especially with things that she couldn't do herself, that in her mind needed to be done – and done now. Things like putting the clothes in the airing cupboard in order rather than them being in a heap. Sorting out the paperwork that was in the drawer in her living room, which were all old household bills from years gone by. These types of behaviours – putting things in order, clearing out and getting things 'sorted' – are all associated with feeling a sense of control and achievement. They can also be related to achieving closure. It was no surprise to me that Mum was dictating in this way. I simply got on with whatever she asked for.

S-L

The nature of our 'attachment' to things, including our thoughts and abilities, our body and our mind, strongly influences our ability to 'let go'. The stronger the attachment, the harder it is for us to let go. We become attached to people and things because it helps us to feel safe. Through our attachments we 'stabilise' our world, so when those things we are attached to start to change or are taken from us, it destabilises our world. One result of this process is that we experience higher levels of fear and anxiety. When we realise that we truly own nothing, including our body and mind, and that nothing is permanent or stable, we can learn the art of feeling safe while accepting that things will change – which is the art of letting go.

One day I got a call from Nat saying that Mum had just burned all the paperwork that was in the drawer in her front room. Well, technically speaking she hadn't burned it. She had tried to burn it, taking it up to the top of her garden, putting it into her metal bin and trying to set fire to it. One of the neighbours saw her struggling and went to assist. She wasn't able to strike a match and would have been more likely to set fire to herself than the paperwork, so he stepped in and helped. Not realising that the documents in the bin also included her current insurance documents, they were duly disposed of and Mum was content that all was in order.

Although, this really did make me laugh because it was typical of her desire for efficiency and order, I spent the next two weeks trying to work out what had been burned, tracking down the insurance companies and documents that we still needed and getting new documents issued. As anyone who has tried to speak to an insurance company on behalf of someone else knows, this isn't always a simple process, especially when you don't have a policy number to give them, you are not the policy holder and you don't have an official power of attorney. Thankfully, Mum's insurance company were very understanding, but it was just another task we could have all done without. Mum, of course, couldn't see what all the fuss was about. She burned her old documents every year! Mum was definitely not of sound mind and things weren't going to get any easier as time went on. The problem at this point was that Mum still thought she was completely of sound mind. The challenge was becoming one of not undermining her and what she was saying, so that she still felt some element of control and independence, while also making sure she had the appropriate care and attention that she needed.

> *The illusion of hope can blind us to the reality of the situation and lead to denial.*

Mum was in a reasonably good place, which was a relief to us all. Her symptoms were quite stable again, any deterioration was happening slowly and she seemed settled in herself and her home. It would have been easy to think that she could go on for a few years this way, but that would have been an illusion of hope and not the reality of the situation. The reality was that every day was different. The Iain Rennie and community nurses were excellent throughout this process. They have a really tough job to strike the balance of allowing someone to live the best they can, while also getting them to acknowledge that they are dying, in order that they can prepare themselves and their families for that eventuality. It is an emotionally charged situation for all parties involved. They needed to ask Mum certain difficult questions; for example, about her desire for resuscitation, and advise her to make sure her will and personal documentation was in order, at a time when she was feeling that she could go on for years! Mum didn't take too kindly to such questions and became very aggressive towards anyone, including family, who would talk to her in that way. There was a time and a place for such discussions and in Mum's mind now was neither the time nor the place. The Iain Rennie nurse frequently asked me whether I thought Mum was accepting of the fact that she was dying. I said to the nurse that I was absolutely sure that she was aware of the fact that she was dying, but that she wasn't going to let anyone tell her when that would happen. I didn't see any harm in her planning for the winter and Christmas. Time would tell and with time the situation would become undeniable, even to mum.

Mum would get very frustrated when she couldn't do the things she expected to, but this was also part of her character. It was just accentuated by the fact that it was the simple things that she couldn't do anymore. Mum was a fighter and this caused her considerable distress. I suppose it is also a clear sign that things are not right, which makes any form of self-denial more difficult to maintain. Resistance to the truth cannot be sustained under deteriorating health.

At another level Mum was also very fascinated by the fact that she couldn't do the things she used to be able to do. She became really aware of the power of her brain and was somewhat in awe of it. She often asked me why she wasn't able to do things and talked about how much concentration it took for her to do the simple things. I didn't have any specific answers to her questions but would chat generally about how the brain worked and the fact that the tumour, swelling and the drugs she was taking were all having an effect on her brain's ability to function normally. She was being introduced to a science she hadn't considered before. For her generation, it wasn't really commonplace to understand how your body worked, because that was the GP's job, let alone understanding how your brain worked. Mum was intrigued and I am sure spent many hours pondering that topic.

S-L

In order to cope with our loss of independence we must accept the changes we are experiencing. When our fear is strong, so is our fight, and acceptance is then unattainable. Acceptance, though, does not mean to give up. Acceptance, in this context, means to work with these inevitable changes rather than to fight them. When we do this we can give our energy and attention to what is still possible and be present with our current experience, rather than try to force something that we desire and which is impossible – which is to maintain the past. That is not to say that we do not give our energy to improve or repair our health – it is to say we simply suspend our idea of what we used to be able to do and put our efforts into getting the best out of what we can do, given the changes in abilities and functioning. When this is done through the energy of acceptance, our frustration is reduced and our gratitude and appreciation is increased.

Mum sought great solace in her garden; being in it, working on it and enjoying the fruits of her labour, and never did she enjoy it more than in this month of June. She had a vegetable patch at the bottom of her garden and in the spring Helen had planted some things for her. Mum was able to go and tend to things as best she could. Strawberries were coming through thick and fast and the apple tree was loaded with fruit ready for ripening. She had a chair at the bottom of the garden, next to her vegetables, the apple tree and some chickens, which belonged to Helen. Mum would sit up there and enjoy the quiet country air… and ponder. What exactly she pondered, who knows? I suspect, sometimes, she pondered what life was all about and whether hers had been worth it. These were two things she raised with me as we sat together one evening.

Mum was no longer spending money on clothes so she turned her attention to things for the garden. Fortunately, the things she fell in love with were not expensive items. Her wonderful neighbours would take her to a local garden centre where they sold 'seconds'. Mum would be attracted to things that looked worn out and in need of care and attention. One such object was a stone statue of a little girl, with a basket at her feet and two butterflies; one on her arm and the other on the basket. That little girl became the object of Mum's attention as she considered how exactly to repair and decorate her.

During June I went away on holiday. There was of course a part of me that didn't want to go, but I was also confident that Mum was in an okay place and she insisted that I go. Actually, it was the wedding of Murielle's sister, Maz and her fiancé Andy, and it was taking place in Cyprus. I had never been to Cyprus despite spending 12 years in the Army at a time when Cyprus was a popular posting. So, we went out there for a week's holiday with Murielle's parents, Andy's parents and a couple of Maz and Andy's friends. It was a small wedding, very picturesque and very typically Maz and Andy. The wedding itself was glamorous, luxurious and so very different from our own wedding in December. It was a wonderful 5* hotel with sunshine and temperatures in the high 20s. We stayed in a villa outside the main hotel complex and there was a small swimming pool close to our accommodation. We had been taking Amelie to Waterbabies from the age of 12 weeks, which is a brilliant swimming group for babies, and she absolutely loved the water. This was a fabulous opportunity for us to have fun and keep Amelie entertained at the same time. We took her into the swimming pool every day and she had an amazing time. It is so wonderful to watch a young baby grow in confidence and water is a great place to achieve that. Although the wedding was lovely, being with Amelie was the most fun part of the week for Murielle and I, who were so in awe of our little girl's progress that we probably bored people with our incessant reflections!

I was texting Mum a couple of times a day, keeping her informed of what we were up to. I felt (and Mum agreed) that it was important for me to share the details of what I was doing because it helped her to have something outside of her world to give her attention to, in order to maintain some aspect of normality. My little updates included what we had done and a description of Cyprus and the people. She wasn't able to text back any words, but we had agreed our own signal. She would send me a blank text back and I would know she had received my message.

About three days into the holiday Mum phoned me. This was unexpected, and it would be costing her as she only had a pay-as-you-go phone. So I called her back. Mum was really very chirpy and she said that she had really been enjoying my messages and she just wanted to hear my voice. My heart sank as once again I had that strong realisation that the amount of time I had left to hear her voice was reducing. I have to say, such realisations feel less distressing when you are sitting in the wonderful warm sunshine, overlooking gorgeous scenery. Nonetheless it was a struggle to hold back the tears and talk as if life was carrying on as normal. I continued to text mum and phoned her a couple of times to update her on the food and reminisce with her over our family holiday to Greece when I was in my 20s. I knew she would be able to relate to that and hoped it gave her some comfort.

Needless to say, I couldn't wait to get back to Mum, yet at the same time it was a desperately needed break for me and Murielle. Looking after Mum was taking its toll, but I wouldn't have been able to do it any other way. I knew deep down inside that we would all come through it, with time, which was something she didn't have a great deal of. Murielle was brilliant and I couldn't have gone through it without her.

Back from the wedding and Mum was still in good form. We used to go food shopping regularly, which would easily take a couple of hours. Mum loved to get out and about. It made her feel human again and normality was achieved that way. Nat, bless her, was still looking after Mum in the week and I would go over there on Friday and stay until Monday. Mum was still very demanding, but at least able to get to and from the loo on her own. She wasn't able to cook for herself now, as a result of her nearly setting fire to the house when she forgot she had put a steak on the hob, gone and sat on her bed and fallen asleep! This incident wasn't the first time she had left something to burn and it wasn't the last either. Mum's desire to still cook for herself was admirable, but it became a source of concern for us all. It was the danger to herself that was more of an issue than the symptoms of her condition during this period of time. It was a time when she was still mobile and able to do some things, yet significantly impaired by the drugs she was taking and the changing functioning of her brain.

Forgetting, confusion, disorientation are all key symptoms which of themselves are not a problem, insofar as you can work with them as a carer. They become a problem though when accompanied by physical mobility, as Mum could get into some serious problems. She would fiddle with things and then forget she had done so. At one point she had no hot water and heating. On another occasion I came downstairs at 2 a.m. to find her drinking a cup of cold tea that she thought she had boiled the kettle for. It was very sad to see the deterioration, whilst at the same time needing to deal with the practical safety and reality, which required a pragmatic and objective approach. It felt like an emotional cocktail and was a source of anxiety between us, as Mum strongly resisted the idea that she wasn't allowed to cook any more. The answer was… Indian takeaway!

S-L

Pragmatism and objectivity are used as ways of avoiding the negative emotions inherent in challenging situations. They are the mental tools necessary for handling crisis situations (such as war and disaster) and involve the skill of observing from a detached perspective in order that our emotions do not interfere with our decisions and subsequently influence our actions. The art of detachment can be trained, but it can also happen spontaneously as a function of being thrust into a position of having to mentally function within a highly emotionally charged situation (such as dealing with death and post-death administration). When we are thrust into detachment in this way rather than trained for it, we must be sure that we exit from it once the situation has changed. If we don't, this type of detachment can lead to dysfunctional emotional responses and disengagement from life.

Friday night became Indian takeaway night for Mum and me. She had an Indian restaurant close to her home and that became our main meal of the week to share together. Mum would have her king prawn balti and I'd have chicken dansak. We shared the sag aloo, rice and naan bread. Mum was in heaven and I was stuffed. Mum had an appetite that was never satisfied. She was able to polish off most of the food (thankfully for me) and then would tuck into strawberries and cream. I buried my head in the white wine instead, which I was fully aware wasn't going to solve the problem, but after a couple of glasses I didn't care either!

Strawberries, raspberries and cream became a daily ritual and Mum loved it. From this moment we moved her on to ready meals and discovered some wonderful food that could either be eaten cold or was easy for her to heat up in the microwave. No more worries about burning the house down. The Friday night Indian was accompanied by the first two series of *Gavin & Stacey*. I had never seen these series and Mum loved it. It was fun and a great escape. Humour is such a wonderful tonic.

The steroids were clearly having an effect. Mum would spend most nights awake. She would spend the night watching television. I would hear her moving around in the night and always had to keep one ear open, just in case she fell. Sometimes she would get up simply to go to the loo, but at other times she would think the middle of the night was morning and be making herself breakfast at 2.30. Often she would drop something. The smashing sound would be followed by, 'Bugger!' I would rush downstairs and find Mum stood, stuck to the floor, unable to know how to move and physically shaking. 'It's alright mum,' I would say. 'Would you like a cup of tea? I'll make it for you. Let's get you back into bed.' Sometimes she would thank me and apologise, and sometimes she would swear and curse at me as if I was to blame, which was perfectly understandable. I am sure I would have done the same in her position. I just gave her a hug, escorted her back to bed and then went about clearing up the mess and making her a hot cup of tea. A cup of tea often solved the problem, at least temporarily. Mum was getting bigger and her movement was becoming more challenging. Her legs in particular were very swollen and she couldn't get comfortable.

All in all, the month of June was probably Mum's best month. We were able to get more glimpses of 'Mum' than in previous months. She was in good humour. She was entrenched in the tennis at Wimbledon and still enjoying a wide range of television programmes. The steroids made her feel on top of the world for the most part. The downside was the sleepless nights, but this didn't seem to affect mum a great deal. The swelling was starting to negatively affect her mobility because it creates a weakness in the thigh muscles which means your legs don't work properly, but that was a small price to pay for a short spell of quality of life. The summer was in full flow and Mum was able to really enjoy the wonderful flowers in her garden. She felt safe and comfortable and, but for the odd lapse into frustration with her inability to do simple tasks, she was as content as she could be.

Spiritual-Logic Insights

Engaging with our Spiritual-Logic is to become totally at one with the impermanent nature of all things including ourself.

To learn to truly love we must let go of our unhealthy dependent attachments and engage in healthy co-dependent relationships. This means we live with an appreciation of our need for others and their need for us, but without exercising power and control over others and without threatening them through guilt or blame.

When we recognise our fears for what they are, and cease to take them seriously, we will free ourselves from the constraints of our past unhelpful conditioning. Nothing can guarantee our physical safety in this world – at some point we will physically die and before that time comes we will have experienced a number of other more subtle, psycho-emotional, deaths: rejection; humiliation; betrayal; abandonment; the killing of our ideas by someone; emotional abuse such as 'put-downs'; not feeling listened to or appreciated; or feeling under-valued by someone – and we will have played our own part in administering these subtle deaths in others.

Death is of course a natural part of the cycle of life. Something needs to die in order for something new to be created. We need to kill off our old unhelpful beliefs and thoughts in order to replace them with more helpful ones. None of this, though, is anything other than our human experience. How we handle these aspects of our journey in life – the rejection and humiliation – determines the way in which we are able to cope with our own physical death (assuming we get the chance to do so) and how we handle the death of others. With each small death we can either re-grow stronger, wiser and better able to cope, or we can wither and die a little inside each time. Stop for a moment and ask the questions, 'who am I?' and 'who are they?' How we define ourself defines our destiny. How we define others, defines how we relate to them. To change our destiny and how we relate, we need to change how we define ourself! When we define ourself by our acquisitions, status, money, knowledge, authority and role there is a tendency for us to form strong attachments to these things. When they are subsequently withdrawn from us we feel the pain. We can become attached to our independence, control, our needs and our problems. These things become a part of our character to the extent that we can find them difficult to let go of. But, who are we really? We are all these things and yet we are none of these things at the same time. Everything is as it is and nothing has meaning except that which we assign to it. To give appropriate meaning is Wisdom, and Wisdom is to let go.

Developing Spiritual-Logic

✓ Accept that every day will be different throughout a terminal illness. The changing mind of a dying person is a reflection of their inner processing and depreciation in functioning, and something we need to learn to work with and accept rather than challenge or correct.

✓ Always actively strive to include someone who is dying, in life, rather than exclude them or isolate them from life. They are dying, they are not dead, yet!

✓ Be prepared to be flexible and stay calm with the changing nature of things. You cannot have fixed plans as these will only lead to frustration.

✓ If someone who is dying is frustrated, it is most likely that they feel out of control – work together to help them feel in control of the things that they are able to control, and accepting of the things that they cannot.

✓ Do not avoid negative feelings or prevent a dying person from expressing them. Embrace each emotion as it arises and learn to work with it. It's not about liking it, it's about developing your Spirit and Soul as a result of fully experiencing the moment.

Was My Life Worth Something? – July 2011

Mum and I chatted a lot when I was with her at the weekends. It was easier without Amelie there. Mum was becoming less able to cope with Amelie, who by now was walking and was into everything. If she came with me to Mum's, Mum would get tired very quickly, so my visits with Amelie reduced. Sometimes, when we talked we just reflected on normal day-to-day events and sometimes Mum would talk in a way that made me very aware that she knew she was not long for this world. On one occasion she had clearly been reviewing her life, as I am sure I would do in her situation. In a way it was wonderful when Mum had those moments of real lucidity. During these times we were the closest we had ever been and there was a sense of calmness and acceptance within her. We had conversations that were just one human being to another: no pretence, no show, no hiding, no protecting, no role-playing, just pure open discussion about what was happening.

I suppose it was at these times that Mum really shared her feelings and thoughts. It is difficult for me to describe, but there was a sense of purity about these conversations: pure acceptance of everything that had happened, was happening and was going to happen, and pure forgiveness for anything that shouldn't have happened in the past. There was a real acknowledgment between us of the fact that we are all fallible human beings doing the best we can to survive and be happy. Mum showed her sadness in these moments, which I found the most challenging of situations. She didn't want to die and wasn't ready to die, but she knew she was dying. To this day I still don't know how you handle that.

Even though Mum was severely disabled by her condition, she would have taken as many years as you would have given her with that disability rather than leave the life that she was enjoying so much. She still had so much to live for. These were heart-breaking moments, yet moments of total honesty and openness. Strangely, I was left with an even stronger connection and faith. It was as if these moments of closeness were playing some part in repairing my broken heart.

> *We are all fallible human beings doing the best we can to survive and be happy.*

S-L

When we forgive others (and ourself), we let go of the negative energy that we were holding in relation to them (or us). Of course, when we don't forgive, we are the one doing the 'holding' of negative energy, inside ourself, and this negative energy can do a great deal of damage to our body, mind and

Spirit. When we choose not to forgive – we choose the path of revenge, which can only reinforce our experience of emotional pain and suffering. Forgiveness leads to inner peace.

Mum's main concern was whether her life had been worth it. She wasn't talking from the perspective of what she had got out of her life. Materialism wasn't something Mum ever got sucked into. What was really important in her life was her family. Whether by intuition or by experience, she knew it was what she had achieved in the context of her family that mattered, not what she had got out of it. I said that she must have done a fantastic job given she produced four very well adjusted children, which was no mean feat in this world. We laughed at the idea of exactly how well adjusted we all were or weren't.

Mum started to tell me stories of our relatives on her side of the family. This was something she had never talked about before, probably because it had never occurred to her to talk about it. She talked about how intelligent and well-off some of our family were, not that many generations ago. She was not bragging, she was demonstrating to herself that we were from 'good stock'. One had gone to Westminster for his schooling. Another travelled to Australia and discovered Alice Springs. Mum's grandfather, started the London to Brighton bus company. I heard tales of our history I had not been aware of. Some of the tales explained a few things too… in a good way of course.

Mum talked with a sense of fondness and pride, and a realisation that perhaps she hadn't done a bad job after all. Circumstances had led her down a particular route in her own life but in her mind it was clear she had brought into this world four pretty smart children who were very capable of looking after themselves and considerate to others. She couldn't ask for more. She was now satisfied, she had made a positive contribution to this world. This was of more comfort to her than I could have conceived and reinforced my own belief that what we put into this life is worth far more than what we get out of it. Mum seemed to reach a level of contentment and acceptance as a result of her belief that she had done a good job.

> *What we put into this life is worth far more than anything we get out of it.*

S-L

Your gravestone, if you have one, is very unlikely to list your promotions, trophies, final salary and bonuses. There is probably a good reason this is the case!

Nat, understandably, was beginning to struggle with acting as Mum's carer and needed to find herself paid work again. Mum's condition was beginning to show more signs of deterioration and her mobility was suffering. She now needed help with washing and dressing and it wasn't something Nat or I could deal with. It was time to increase the specialist nursing care that Mum was receiving, and time for Nat and I to take a step back and become her daughters again. The difficulty was breaking this news to Mum, who had gained great comfort from our involvement. She didn't take the news too well, but recognised that Nat needed to earn money. Of course, in the first instance, Mum reasoned that she would be able to look after herself and didn't need any additional support. Oh how I wished that had been true, but it was far from it.

The nurses were scheduled to come in three times a day to coincide with washing, mealtimes and to give Mum her medication. One or the other of us would still try and stay overnight if we could, but it wasn't always possible for us to do that.

In some ways, though, the situation now was easier than the previous month because Mum was less mobile and she was receiving specialist attention. But in other ways it was even more challenging. Mum hated the fact that the nurses were 'invading her space', as she used to say and complained bitterly at the way she was treated by them. Again, Mum was being presented with evidence of her deterioration and still resisting the idea that she needed help. Unfortunately for the nurses they took the brunt of it. It was okay for family to help her, but not outsiders. This placed a lot of emotional strain on us all. We still had to keep track of her medication, set it out for the nurses to issue and arrange for any repeat prescriptions to be prepared and collected. This in itself may not sound like a big deal, but when you have six different medications, to be taken in different doses and at different times of the day, and you have to allow 48 hours for a repeat prescription to be issued, and all the pills run out at different times, and then the dose changes as a result of a doctor's visit, it takes a bit of managing. Mum was under strict instructions not to touch her pills at all on the basis that she was now well beyond being mentally capable of following instructions without something going amiss. It was now a bit like a military operation. We were in constant contact with the Iain Rennie nurses, specialist community nurses and the GP surgery.

Mum was still able to get out and about a bit. At least once a week I would go and pick her up and bring her over to Chesham. We would park as close as we could to the town centre and she would walk to Costa Coffee. Costa Coffee became the place to be and Mum fell in love with the latte again. She would walk very, very slowly from the car park to the coffee shop, which is about 500 yards. Now using two sticks, very carefully placed before she could move her legs, this process took a long time. Our trips to Costa and the supermarket were now taking over four hours. Mum needed to stop every few paces to get her breath back. When she stopped she would often lose concentration and even forget where we were going. We persisted together. Sometimes she would get frustrated with me, as I would be chatting away and break her concentration. When that happened her balance was thrown completely and it frightened her. It frightened me too. How she never ended up on the ground at some points I really don't know, but I am grateful that she didn't.

We would sit in Costa and Mum would chat away. Sometimes what she said made sense and sometimes I didn't have a clue what she was talking about. I just went along with her and when I did speak I kept it simple. We used to talk about Jakk becoming a mother. Mum was so proud of Jakk. 'She will make an excellent mother,' she would say. 'I never thought she would be the one to have children,' she would tell me again.

S-L

In an ever-changing landscape there is nothing to grab hold of that is secure and stable. We must create that stability and security by embracing the uncertainty, without feeling threatened or fearful of what might be. All will be as it is. It is how we navigate 'what is' that determines who we become and therefore our contribution in this world.

Jakk had taken mum to see her 20-week scan. Mum was over the moon and especially because the baby had a wonderful head. Mum's fondness for babies' heads will remain with me for sure. 'It looks just like Mike,' mum would say. 'How wonderful, that is fantastic, they will love it and they will be fantastic parents,' I said and we both agreed. I knew the birth of Jakk and Mike's baby was a target Mum had in her mind to see, but at this point in time I don't think any of us were under the illusion that she would see it. Thank heavens for modern technology. Mum had seen her second grandchild on the scan. That was of some comfort to all of us.

The twins had their birthday and we went out for lunch with Mum. We went to a beautiful gastropub that served great food. Mum was very cantankerous and positively rude. This was a particular mood that had developed as a result of her condition and it was a challenge to be around her when she was so stroppy. Nothing was right, until we started eating! Mum had ordered a prawn salad starter that included avocado, mango and some other wonderful ingredients, and fish and chips for her main. The rest of us just ordered a main course. Mum's starter arrived and she tucked in. This was the best food she had ever tasted. She was in heaven and she wanted more of this, so she ordered a main course of the same prawn salad. Now she had two main meals to eat. She tucked into the second salad as if she had never eaten the first and was really enjoying every mouthful. It was good to see mum take pleasure out of something and it didn't matter what it was, how it came about, or what it cost. Those things became irrelevant at moments like this. The most important point was that she was happy enjoying the present moment. She polished off the second salad but only ate some of the fish and chips in order to save herself for pudding! Sticky toffee pudding and ice-cream rounded off the meal nicely and that was that. How mum managed to walk out after eating all that I don't know. What was wonderful though was the fact that she talked about that prawn salad again and again. We were all now on a mission to track down the same salad so that she could have it at home. Well done Marks & Spencer and Waitrose. They saved our bacon.

Mum's increasing frustration with her decreasing independence was hard for all of us to see, because we knew what it meant to her, but I am sure that no one felt it more than Mum herself. The nurses were brilliant and very respectful in helping her to maintain her independence for as long as possible. The guiding principle though is always personal safety. The intention was that Mum was to remain in her own house for as long as possible and ideally until the end. But the last thing any of us wanted was for her to fall over and end up in hospital with a broken hip.

Mum turned her attention back to her little girl in the garden, who was in need of repair. I have come to believe that we create signposts for ourselves, or targets, which serve to maintain our motivation and drive and in terminal situations give us something to live for. The film *The Bucket List* classically represents this. Sometimes the completion of things can therefore represent an acceptance, and facilitate the process, of letting go. Mum had been pondering for a long time how to deal with the little girl in the back garden. In the meantime, she had spent a long time painting her birdhouses.

Each birdhouse now had a green box with a brown lid. She had spent ages over the previous couple of weeks rubbing down the boxes and re-painting them, even giving a them a striped effect on the roof. They looked wonderful. Mum was no artist, she was simply expressing her connection with nature and her desire to make her garden into something special for her own enjoyment. She had saved her most prized work – her little girl – until last.

We create signposts for ourselves, or targets, which serve to maintain our motivation and drive, and give us something tangible to live for.

S-L

If we are blessed, we may get the chance to say goodbye to someone we love, but maybe we won't. What is important is that we let go of any negativity towards others in the moment it arises and share our joyful moments with love and connection. If we don't, then guilt, shame, regret and sadness can haunt us. That which haunts us then becomes our projection in life, which will inevitably cause pain and suffering.

Mum's mobility was becoming significantly impaired and she knew it. I am under no illusion that she knew she only had a short time to complete the restoration of that little girl. She had now made a decision as to how she would do it. I brought the little girl indoors and Mum set to work. She filled the bits that were in need of repair and then started painting. On one of our shopping trips mum had picked up the colours she wanted to use. A gorgeous deep violet blue and dark pink were perfect for the job. Nail varnish was the medium. Mum spent hours carefully repairing the little girl, then leaving her to set. She still had to plan how and where to place the colours. The butterflies had to be done in the blue colour. It took Mum ages to get the painting done because every action was an effort. Even the act of standing to do it was effortful. Mum wasn't going to stop until she was finished. Her determination was to be admired. The finishing of that little girl was like a marker in the sand. It was done and looked like a work of art. That was one more thing off the bucket list and probably the last thing on Mum's bucket list that actually involved her needing to do anything physical.

> *Determination can drive us beyond our boundaries, but faith really does move mountains.*

I popped in one day and Mum was in high spirits. She was sitting on her bed as was often the case and looking out of her window. She turned to me and said, 'I've just seen Grandma. Would you believe it? She came in and stood right there. She had her blue coat on and I could see her as clear as day. Isn't that wonderful? She said everything will be alright.' Mum was so happy and so at peace that I think she could have quite literally died in that moment and would have been in heaven. Whether Grandma appeared or not is not of importance or relevance. What is important, is the fact that Mum felt a great sense of connection and comfort from this experience. For me, it was an indicator that Mum had just a bit more acceptance of the fact that she would be joining her mother at some point soon. For many people, it is the idea of joining the people they loved who have left before them that enables them to achieve a sense of peace as they are dying. Whether we do or not is irrelevant and there is little purpose in debating the issue.

Mum developed a little skill that she was beginning to perfect. She called it her 'sliding to the floor' routine. In the last couple of weeks Mum had been found on the floor. Initially, one of the neighbours had seen her in her garden. She very simply bent over to pick something up and 'slid gracefully' as she put it, to the ground. The problem was not so much that she caused herself a problem falling, more that she couldn't get up. Over the coming weeks though, her legs were showing more signs of not supporting her and on several occasions she was found on the floor. The nurses were becoming concerned, as were we. Mum was in denial about it. She knew that if she owned up to this one she would have to admit defeat and who knows where that would lead!

During this time the Iain Rennie nurses once again stressed to Mum the importance of her personal safety and they tried really hard to help her accept that she was no longer safe doing the things she used to do. They also asked some more difficult questions. They were clear with Mum that they wanted her to remain at home, but at that moment she wasn't helping her own case. If she persisted she would end up either in a nursing home or in hospital with an injury. Mum got the message loud and clear. From that moment onwards Mum was very complimentary about the Iain Rennie nurses. 'What they were saying was very true,' she said, and she definitely wanted to stay at home. Mum apologised to us for being inconsiderate.

I never thought of her as being inconsiderate at all. I think Mum was trying to live her life the best she could for as long as possible and I for one wasn't going to stop her doing that. I was certainly fearful of her doing herself an injury and I knew there would come a point when she would be forced to stop. That point was about to happen.

Spiritual-Logic Insights

Engaging with our Spiritual-Logic is to take advantage of every moment that we have, with gratitude and joy. Not to be obsessed with our desires for something other than that which we have, but to engage with and appreciate the simple things in our life. Simplicity ignites the heart and complexity is the mind's weakness. When we align with our purpose in life, simplicity becomes the normality for us and complexity is nonexistent.

Our smallest contributions generate more impact than we can ever imagine, because to imagine this would require us to wake up to the immense power we actually possess and that is one of the most frightening realisations we can have.

When we engage with our innate power through awareness and love, we live with respect for all things, with an open heart and mind. We can literally move mountains and still we remain humbled by the opportunities that come our way, rather than blinded by our individual sense of achievement.

When we fail to recognise our power we limit ourself and others. We live in fear, build walls to protect what we think we own, and believe that what we have achieved is of great value, because we cannot see that we have only just tapped into the tip of the iceberg.

Developing Spiritual-Logic

✓ Value the smallest things that you do with a dying person every day. Do not dismiss them as being 'nothing'. They all add up, and positively impact their wellbeing and enhance the quality of their life.

✓ Watch for the signposts that the dying person is putting in place and allow them to be. Do not force change on them because this is to take control away. Allow them to come to terms with the changes as time progresses.

- ✓ Help someone who is dying to really appreciate their own contribution right up to the end of their life, to feel that their life did and still does matter and it did and will continue to make a difference. It's not about you, its all about them.
- ✓ Allow your heart to be broken, you will come through it, because love never dies, it is ever-present.
- ✓ Do not hold grudges against anyone involved in the process. Either talk to them about it, or forgive them and yourself for being fallible human beings and let it go. It serves no one to hold on to anger and unfulfilled expectations.

Sliding – August 2011

Mum had taken on board the nurses' concerns regarding her mobility. In actual fact, I think things were running their natural course. Mum knew that painting the little girl was one of her final physical acts. Her mobility was seriously affected now and she was struggling to lift her legs onto the bed. This meant that she would get stuck. Stuck sitting on the bed or sitting on the sofa. The consequences though were significant.

It was Amelie's first birthday on the 10th August. It was certainly an event that I didn't think Mum would ever see. She had asked me to get Amelie a present on her behalf. Mum wanted to be the person to get Amelie her first pair of wellington boots. Another one of Mum's little amusements, like babies' heads. I found a pair of pink wellies that would be right for Amelie for the coming winter and Mum was delighted. I was also tasked to get her a toy of some sort that she could leave at Mum's house for when she visited. We decided on a bucket on wheels with bricks in it. Amelie in all honesty was a bit young for that toy, but Mum was happy. Amelie loves that toy now and plays with it lots… just not at Grandma's house.

I took Amelie round to Mum's on her birthday. My visits with Amelie were rare now because Mum was struggling more and more with the hyperactivity of a small child. Mum was slowing down, and fast movements around her were destabilising for her. It was a struggle for me too. It took more than one adult to handle a 1-year old and Mum at the same time. Mum thanked me for bringing Amelie to see her. 'She is the sunshine in my life,' she said, so no matter how she was feeling, Mum loved seeing Amelie and it was a gift for me to be able to share with Mum too. A child was something neither of us thought would have happened, but I am so grateful it did.

S-L

Seeing a new young life starting its journey of discovery, can lighten our world as it takes us out of our own mind and we can then see the beauty that is before us. Babies, pets, nature, all offer us this outlet – if we really want to engage with it.

Murielle and I went round together one day, which always made things easier because it meant that Mum could see Amelie just enough and also I could spend time with Mum. Mum sat on the edge of the bed. We had all been chatting. Mum wanted some music put on. She wanted to listen to Josh Groban singing 'You Raise Me Up'. It was one of her favourite songs and he was one of her favourite artists. Josh Groban has one of the most special voices of all time and listening to him sing this song wasn't going to be easy for me to handle.

On it went and Mum started singing along with Josh. She started crying as she was singing, telling me how she had always had faith and it was her faith that had got her through all the bad times in her life. It was her faith that had got her through the last few months… I was in bits, crying my eyes out and I looked across at Murielle who was also bawling. Mum said, 'I want this song at my funeral.' I just said, 'yes Mum.' We cried together for the first time, but not the last time.

Mum's legs weren't working. One morning I got a call to say that she'd fallen over in her house. She had been found by the nurse that morning and she had badly banged her head. One of Mum's neighbours worked for the NHS ambulances and was helping to get her back onto her bed. Mum was okay and chatting as if nothing had happened. I rushed over. She couldn't remember a thing. She had no idea how she had ended up on the floor and at some points didn't even know that she had been on the floor. All she did know was that the back of her head was sore. The bruising on Mum's head was significant and extended down the back of her neck. We will never know whether she blacked out, which can happen with a tumour, or her legs simply gave way and she slid to the floor. Either way she slid to the floor with a bang. The GP came round and gave Mum the all-clear. It was now clear that Mum was unlikely to be able to stay in her home for very much longer.

A week later I picked up an answerphone message from Mum. 'Where are you, I am on the fucking floor and you are not here.' Then immediately following that message, another message. 'Where are you, I can't get up, why have you left me like this?' My heart hit the floor again. I had to think quickly. It was about 9 p.m. I phoned the Iain Rennie nursing team to let them know and they said they would call an ambulance. When someone is on the floor, the ambulance crew are technically the only people who can lift the person. I knew I wouldn't be able to lift Mum on my own and I knew she was well enough to be cursing at me down the phone. I then called Helen. Thankfully she answered her phone and immediately recruited her husband and Mum's other neighbour, with his lifting gear, round to Mum's. They had been having a BBQ together so it was no bother. I phoned Mum and spoke to her. She was laughing and telling me about 'sliding to the floor' again. She was very put out that so many people had descended upon her house and couldn't see what all the fuss was about. 'And how on earth did these ambulance people get here?' she said. 'That's ridiculous,' she said. She had completely forgotten that she had called me. I spoke to Helen who reassured me it was all under control. I went to bed thinking, 'Mum is now unsafe, what are the options?'

The Iain Rennie nurses went to visit Mum the following day and she admitted that she was not safe at home any more. Her legs were significantly swollen. They were giving way on her and as a result she would find herself stuck. This could easily mean that she would be stuck in a sitting position on the end of her bed for the whole night. That was not acceptable and certainly not safe. To add to matters we were

what to do. Some might call this manipulation, others persuasion, others would just say it is effective communication. For a person to feel that they have made a decision of their own volition, and when the doing so facilitates their feeling of control and wellbeing, cannot be a bad thing.

Mum was frustrated on the journey in the car. Again, her frustration when something was changing was nothing new. She had always been uncomfortable with change even before she got sick. So, under these conditions it was inevitable that she would react in this way. The journey took about an hour from Mum's house. We chatted quietly, talking about the wonderful countryside we were going through and she calmed down a little bit. We drove up the long driveway to the Sue Ryder Centre in Nettlebed; a most majestic country house in beautiful grounds. What an amazing and fantastic use of this property. The atmosphere inside the place was serene. Peace and tranquility and respect summed up my experience of the Centre. We were placed in a room that had two beds in it. One bed was occupied and it was clear to me that the lady was indeed dying. I hoped that Mum didn't give her too much attention and within a short time one of the nurses came in and closed off her bed to give both patients the privacy they needed. I had never seen a dying person before – I mean someone who is literally hours away from death – but I recognised this lady was in that place. She wasn't there when I went back to see Mum the following day.

The doctors came and asked Mum some questions, took all her details and welcomed her to the hospice. They asked her what she expected from her visit and it was agreed that they would be looking to sort out her medication. Mum was happy, if only briefly. Then that question came around again. 'Mrs Emms, we have to ask you this… in the event that your heart stops do you want to be resuscitated?' Well, Mum's face was a picture. She looked at me as if astounded and indignant that she had been asked such a stupid question. 'Why are they asking me this?' she said. 'I don't even know how to answer this question, it isn't even on the horizon,' she said. 'How can you expect me to answer this right now?' I looked back at her and said, 'Mum, remember when Grandma was really poorly in hospital and you had to make that decision for her? What the Doctor needs to know is, if you are in that state, would you want them to resuscitate you. It would have to be really bad for that to happen,' I said. 'No,' she said. Job done. The doctors had the answer they needed and we could move on.

They moved Mum into a room on her own, which we were grateful for and she started the process of settling in. Only one problem… Mum had envisioned that she was going on a sort of holiday retreat, which in her mind also meant that she would be able to get out and about around the grounds. She was now under strict instructions not to move on her own, which to be honest she could hardly do anyway. If she needed anything she was to call for a nurse. They didn't want anyone falling over on their shift, the nurse said. Mum was anxious and feeling a little trapped, but at least she had a television. The rest of us, including the neighbours, were relieved. At least Mum was safe and in the best hands.

I went to see Mum pretty much every day. On my second visit, she was sat in the chair by the side of her bed. She looked so lost. I didn't have Amelie with me, which was nice because it gave us a chance to chat. Mum started crying. She sobbed as she said, 'I have never felt so lonely and alone as I feel right now.' I didn't know what to say. I hugged her and softly said, 'I love you mum. I am so sorry.' I think she knew she wasn't going home and it was one of those moments of what I called lucidity that was so very hard to handle, yet connected us at the deepest level. You cannot take away someone's feeling of loneliness. It is one of those things we have to learn to accept. It is a fact that we are all alone and we certainly die alone.

In some of our chats throughout the preceding months one of our little phrases had become 'This wasn't in my plan for 2011'. I have never been an avid goal-setter in my work or life. I don't think goal-setting works that well and what was happening reinforced my views. It makes me wonder what is in the plan and causes me to question how much control we really do have. In that moment Mum had no control and in that moment she was entirely alone.

> *You cannot take away someone's feeling of loneliness.*

S-L

Loneliness is the overwhelming feeling of separation that we experience at the deepest level of our being. It is something that many people fear. It causes us to feel isolated and the feeling of it is also isolating. The truth is that we die alone and to die is to separate ourself from others. No one can be there with us (not really with us) in these moments, because it is our world that is separating from the world of others and it is our mind that has to handle this. Overcoming the feelings of loneliness requires practising the art of acceptance and letting go.

In all our conversations now, the moments of lucidity were over quite quickly, and Mum was back to talking about her plans for going back home. 'How long do you think I will be here?' she said. 'Maybe I will be home in a week, what do you think?' I am not sure which type of conversation was easier to deal with. 'As soon as they have sorted out your medication Mum, then we can find out about going home.' They re-tested for a urine infection, which came up positive. That explained a few things and Mum was feeling a bit more content that something significant in terms of her treatment was taking place. It did make me wonder how the earlier test (only three days earlier) could come up negative! Mum's bloods were good. Mum saw this as a positive sign and was convincing herself that she would be going home soon. She was already disenchanted with this holiday.

On Tuesday 30th August I got a call from Mum. She was over the moon. She had just had a Jacuzzi and was blown away by it. Mum had never had a Jacuzzi before and she wanted one of those every day. It had made her body feel light and just wonderful. I can imagine it must have been a fantastic relief for her body. She was happy again and feeling a little more settled.

Spiritual-Logic Insights

Engaging with our Spiritual-Logic is to learn to handle the duality (or dichotomy) within which we create our world. For us to know that good exists we have to know bad exists too. Our world is designed within this duality and very often we align ourself with one side or the other. Our ability to see this duality for what it is, and select the right tools for the journey we are undertaking in any moment in time, leads to our experience of a greater sense of connectedness to all that is one, inner peace, comfort and of course Wisdom.

Give the gift of empowerment to others in order that they may feel strong and be able to navigate their life and death with less pain and suffering.

In order to experience loneliness (separation) we also have to experience attachment (connection). Therefore, when we learn to let go of our attachments, and to create healthy attachments in which we know and accept that everything must leave us, we train ourself to handle loneliness. This practice is all it takes to be able to work with the duality and develop Spiritual-Logic. It is not easy, but then nothing in life worth anything is!

Developing Spiritual-Logic

- ✓ Always try to help others to feel in control rather than take it from them. They will still need you!
- ✓ If you feel lonely, be at one with it. Don't try to not feel lonely, or force it to go. Just 'be present' with it – by observing it. Trust that it will pass. You cannot take away a dying person's experience of loneliness, but you can be present with them if they are feeling this way.
- ✓ Look for something joyful to celebrate together every day – something that doesn't involve an exchange of money, but involves you and the natural world.
- ✓ Only make decisions for a dying person if they are incapable (medically defined), or if they ask you.
- ✓ Be honest. Do not delude a dying person unless it is purely for their benefit and anything other than this would cause them unnecessary pain and suffering.

You Raise Me Up – September 2011

One day I went over to see Mum and we walked out on to the veranda to look out over the grounds. They were beautiful. There was a small lake surrounded by an expanse of lawn and then rows of trees interwoven by pathways: a typical country estate. Getting Mum outside was in itself a challenge. She had to move around in a wheelchair, as the nurses, rightly so, wouldn't let her use her sticks at all. We had to negotiate the inside balcony which overlooked the foyer area. Mum hated heights at the best of times and manoeuvering around the upper balcony caused her a great deal of anxiety. From there we had to get into a lift to go to the next floor down and then we could get out onto the balcony that overlooked the grounds at the back of the house. Mum pointed out a courtyard area to the left of the property. She told me that this is where they stored furniture and bits that people had gifted and that there was an auction of it at the weekend. 'Perhaps we should see if we can pick up some stuff,' she said. Mum loved to watch the auction programmes on television and the Antiques Roadshow. Now she had her very own auction on her doorstep.

We were standing quietly enjoying the scenery when the bells from the church on the estate started to ring, just beyond the courtyard. 'For whom the bell tolls,' Mum said immediately. 'It tolls for me,' she said. I knew exactly the film Mum was quoting from – we had watched it together many years ago. My heart sank at this truth. 'Yes,' I said, as I held her hand and squeezed it. Most often I couldn't think of anything to say and most often saying nothing was the right thing, but it was also important to acknowledge when Mum was admitting that she was dying. I think it helps more than trying to avoid the truth, no matter how painful it is to hear it. I was always in gentle agreement with Mum when she mentioned such things.

S-L

Unconditional love is the only thing we can give that is consistent and all-powerful. It heals the Soul, soothes the mind and calms the body. It expects nothing in return, which also means we are able to let go of that which we unconditionally love. It breaks down resistance and therefore facilitates acceptance. It is the essence of forgiveness and compassion. It is both our path and our destiny.

Mum wanted to go home. She was adamant she was going home. She was going to make home-made soup, under supervision of course. I was going to supervise her and she promised she would follow my instructions. It was a last ditch attempt to maintain some form of normality and something positive to talk about. Mum had been given soup at the hospice – a range of home-made soups and she loved them. When she fell in love with a food during her illness, she couldn't let it go. She had a passion for pasties and pies in the beginning, strawberries all summer, curry, the prawn salad and now the soup. They had a different soup every day and it became the main topic of conversation. At least this was one conversation that was safe for my fragile heart!

I took Amelie in with me a few times and Mum's eyes sparkled once again. We took Mum's photos in from home, just to make things feel as comfortable as possible. Amelie was running around now and it was never easy keeping her under control while giving Mum the time and attention that she needed. It was important for us to make the effort though because Mum wanted to see Amelie. On the few occasions she wasn't up to seeing her, I didn't take her in or we left very quickly.

The team had been adjusting Mum's medication. The urine infection had cleared and she seemed quite stable. They suggested a meeting to discuss what we needed to do next. We had a meeting with the occupational therapist and the specialist doctor on 9th September. Malc and I attended the meeting and they were talking of us needing to move Mum to a nursing home. She was too well to be in the hospice. It would probably take about 10 days for them to sort out the paperwork. They would investigate who had availability and we would be informed of the options. They asked us whether we thought her condition had changed, on the basis that we were more aware of her progression to date. We both said that we thought Mum had deteriorated significantly in the last two weeks while at the hospice. We said we thought that she was actually sicker than she was letting on. Mum was a master of disguise and while she was still planning her exit strategy home she was able to give a really good impression… to a point. That same day Mum had started to be physically sick. She had also become quieter and less interactive. The doctors admitted it was really difficult to know which way things would go. I was about to go on holiday to Corsica for two weeks.

S-L

Our intuition is more powerful than our mind, which is too heavily conditioned to be free to sense without bias. In order for us to tap into our intuition we first need to know ourself – to separate that which is of the conditioned mind and that which is of our intuitive sense. Then we need to trust ourself to follow our intuition rather than find excellent logical reasons why we shouldn't!

I had been sitting with Mum just before the meeting. She was sitting in the chair, with a bowl on her lap. She was still feeling very sick and had been sick on a number of occasions. She looked rough and was very quiet. I sat as close to her as I could get and started stroking her head, the right hand side of her head, behind which lay the tumour that was slowly taking her life. She didn't look up, she just said in a soft voice, 'It's broken.' 'I know,' I said, softly back. 'You've got to live your life now,' she said. 'Mine is over.' I carried on stroking her head softly for a while before she needed to get back into bed. 'I can't cope with this any more,' Mum said as she struggled to get into bed. She didn't really want any company that day. She felt so sick and it wasn't improving. I knew she wouldn't be going to any nursing home. I was going on holiday the next day for two weeks and I knew in my heart I wouldn't be seeing Mum again.

On Saturday 10th September Murielle, Amelie and I set off for Gatwick Airport. We had agreed to go via Mum. It would be a fleeting visit, but I needed to see Mum just one last time. She was still being sick, not eating anything and, understandably, she didn't want to talk either. She forced herself to say hello to Amelie. We didn't stay long. All I could say to her was, 'Take care sweetie. They are going to sort your drugs out so hopefully the sickness will stop and you will feel a bit better soon. I will call you every day and see you when I get back.' 'I hope so,' Mum mumbled. We left.

S-L

We make choices in our life that we must hold ourselves to be accountable for. We can blame no one, because deep down we know we have free will. Some may criticise our choices, others may agree with them, but at the end of the day it is ourself that we have to live with... and die with.

My sisters and brother visited pretty much every day from Sunday 11th. We arrived in Corsica on that Sunday morning and I immediately texted Nat. She called me back. 'Mum has deteriorated quite a lot overnight,' she said. 'I am going to stay here and may stay overnight. If she gets any worse she may not make it through the night.' I started crying. 'Shall I come back?' I asked. It was a question that only I could answer and it was not an easy decision. The reality was that Mum's condition could deteriorate rapidly or slowly. If it was rapidly I may not get back in time to see her and if it was slowly she could still be there when I got back from holiday. I phoned and spoke to the doctor. Mum had deteriorated, but she wasn't at the final stage yet and she may remain like this for some time. They couldn't tell what would happen, but in their view there was no rush for me to come home. I decided to stay in Corsica. In my mind, if I am honest, I knew before I left that I would stay in Corsica throughout. I called Mum and she managed to mumble a few words to me.

Over the next couple of days I called Mum and we had brief chats. She was at least able to speak, but her spirit was tired. She didn't say many words and the conversations only lasted less than a minute. It was just a matter of time now. I had checked things out on the Internet. There is a very good website that gives a great deal of helpful information: www.braintumor.org. I was aware of the progressions from this point on. Mum was most likely in her last 5-7 days of life.

I called the next day and Mum was on cloud cuckoo. She was on morphine. Jakk and Nat were with her and she was eating. She was as high as a kite, but it didn't matter. She was having a ball eating jelly and ice-cream and telling me all about it, like a child coming back from their friend's birthday party and sharing their excitement with you. It was a lovely respite and clearly drug-induced. It was the last time Mum was able to speak to me. When I called the next day she had deteriorated again. The nurse gave her the phone to speak to me, but it was such an effort and Mum was so tired, she couldn't really say anything. I just said to her, 'alright Mum, I will let you rest a bit and call back later.' She mumbled and I put the phone down. I never spoke to her again. From then on, when I called the nurse just said that she was comfortable.

On Saturday 17th and Sunday 18th I felt very agitated. I couldn't understand why exactly. I phoned daily for updates from the doctors and was told Mum was pretty stable, though deteriorating daily. I thought she had about 2-5 days of life and although I was undecided about going home, in my mind I knew it wouldn't serve any purpose. Mum had told me to live my life and maybe me being away had also given her permission to die. I was constantly praying that she could 'leave' whenever she wanted. In fact I had been praying for Mum to leave for a while now. She had clearly had enough of the situation and it was only going in one direction. The sooner we got there the better as far as I was concerned.

On Monday 19th I felt very calm, almost a sense of contentment. It seems strange to say this. It felt as if Mum's spirit was already with me. On Tuesday morning I called Nat. Mum will be leaving us today. We both agreed. That evening at 7 p.m. I called Nat. While I was on the phone to her the hospice called. Mum had just passed away. We cried together, not for the first time, nor the last. Thank God, for Mum now it was over. I had spoken to Jakk and Nat on the Tuesday to see if they would be okay dealing with the administration that needed to take place before I got back on the Sunday. If not I would come home. I had been checking flights, if only trying to convince myself to go back, but if I had left on the Tuesday I would not have made it in time to see Mum. The girls were okay with sorting the administration out and fully supported my decision to stay in Corsica. I would deal with the funeral arrangements when I got home.

S-L

Eternal peace is a blessing and when someone is suffering with no way back to life, to wish them no further suffering in this world is an act of compassion. We let them go. We let them fly. Free from pain. Yet, we remain connected to them, in Spirit, as if they had never left. This is the best of both worlds.

Mum was with me, of that there was no doubt in my mind. As I sat by the pool in the mountains of Corsica looking out over the valley, I wrote a poem. I say I wrote a poem. I am pretty sure Mum wrote the poem through me. I had decided that I would read the poem at her cremation. It was the end of an era, but not the end of Mum. Her influence will remain in all the people she touched in her life. That is, after all, the essence of our eternity here on earth.

We returned from holiday on Sunday and had a meeting on the Monday morning with the minister delivering the cremation service. We all descended on Jakk's house. Everyone looked ghastly and especially Jakk who was now eight months pregnant. We talked through the format for the ceremony, which would be a simple affair as that's what Mum would have wanted.

Mum had selected the music herself. Malc had brought his laptop so we could hear versions of the songs. Mum had chosen: Josh Groban, 'You Raise Me Up'. Murielle and I had already shared this song with Mum in August. I didn't know how on earth I was going to get through the service, let alone speak! Then Malc revealed the other songs Mum wanted... 'Perhaps Love' by Placido Domingo & John Denver and 'Amazing Grace'. Anyone who knows those songs will already know their emotional impact. They would bring the house down. We settled on the most fantastic version I have heard of 'Amazing Grace', by Declan Galbraith. We were all in tears, including the minister, who was the most wonderfully gentle and compassionate woman I have ever met in my life. The fourth song would at least get people pepped up again. It was 'Have a Drink on Me' by Lonnie Donegan.

Dick, Mum's brother, did the second reading. Bless him, he had to follow the committal and 'Amazing Grace', and since his mum (our grandmother) was called Gracie, getting the words out would be nothing short of a miracle. My reading was to follow Josh Groban! The minister had suggested I do my reading at the beginning so that I could feel free to let go throughout the rest of the ceremony. It was of course the most sensible way round, I just had to get myself past Josh Groban... for Mum. I had been rehearsing the poem almost continuously while in Corsica. I knew it verbatim. That of course is all well and good when you are rehearsing walking round a swimming pool in the sun and overlooking stunning scenery. I was still able to mentally rehearse the idea of the ceremony, which took my rehearsals just a little closer to the reality of what it would be like... but I knew it was going to take a lot more practice under some very different conditions for me to know that I could cope in the moment. Now I knew I was following Josh Groban, and my only thoughts were of Mum sitting on the edge of her bed crying as she was trying to sing the words of this most awesome song, at the same time knowing that she didn't want to die. I was in bits!

S-L

When we bring ourself into present time the only emotion we experience is the one in that moment. It is necessary to train our mind to achieve this – it will not happen in and of itself. When we operate in the present moment there is no suppression of emotion, just a stillness of mind – an absence of thought, an absence of past and future – just total engagement in the silence of the now.

The cremation was scheduled for Wednesday 28th at 11.30 a.m. It was now Monday afternoon. I knew there would be some key moments for me where I would struggle to control the sadness. The first was seeing Mum's coffin at her house. The second was walking in behind the coffin at the crematorium. The third was following Josh Groban. The fourth was the closing of the curtains. The fourth didn't really matter. I could cry my eyes out after I had done my reading. I had to be able to deal with the other triggers though. Mum's house was a good 40 minutes from the crematorium so I knew I would be able to recover myself after seeing her coffin outside the house, so that situation I didn't give too much attention to. Walking in behind the coffin and following Josh Groban were the two key triggers to handle.

I arranged to go to the crematorium on the Tuesday afternoon. Just driving into the grounds I was welling up. When I was shown the room that the service would take place in I could only just control myself. Bless the chap who was showing me around. He was telling me all about the history of the place, which was all well and good, but not really of interest to me in that moment in time. It wasn't even that much of a distraction. My mind was already visualising us walking in behind Mum's coffin and seeing it placed at the front of the room, noticing where the lectern was that I would speak from, and the size and format of the room. We had no real idea of how many people would turn up. The members of Mum's golf club had been informed and I was sure that a good number of them would show up. I wasn't going to let Mum down. This was the last thing I could do for her – give her a good send off.

I came home and put Josh Groban on repeat. I cried and cried and cried and cried. I had to get this out of my system and 'flooding' is one of the techniques that is used for such purposes. I was certainly flooding! I would play the record, stop it, stand up and read the poem. Repeatedly, I must have gone through this process a hundred times. I would stop and do something else for a while, then go back to it, hoping I had made some progress. Nope! The tears came flooding again and again. I put Mum's picture on the computer as well, just to make matters worse, and went again. I visualised walking in behind the coffin, then the music, then standing up and speaking. Again and again I went through the process, let the tears flow and somehow I knew I would be able to do it. I have been fortunate enough to deliver a number of speaking and training events over the years and my military training was coming into full use now. Yet this was by far my toughest speaking challenge yet.

S-L

Trust in oneself involves knowing one's boundaries of skill, together with a willingness to step outside of that space, into whatever exists beyond, with faith that no matter what happens we will handle it. Such faith involves an acceptance of our imperfection and a desire to experience the new (even if that is not comfortable). To handle it, involves an acceptance of the possibility that things may not go as we would wish and to still go, willingly, with the flow. To achieve this we need to override our human logic conditioned responses, such as embarrassment, fear, anxiety and self-consciousness.

We had agreed that there should be only a limited amount of black at the service. Mum would have been pleased with that. She had always said she wanted lots of colour. I wore a pink shirt. There was a great deal of colour in the room and it really helped to lift the mood. This should be a celebration of a life that had touched many people. In spite of our sadness there was also a relief that Mum wasn't suffering any more. That in itself was worth celebrating. I cried when I saw Mum's coffin arrive outside her house. It was the most glorious sunny day and in fact quite warm for late September. Malc was following the hearse on his black Harley Davidson. Mum never liked him having bikes that much because she was always concerned he would kill himself, but she loved that bike. She had even asked him to take her for a ride on it during the summer... it was probably another one of those bucket list experiences. Clearly it never happened, but it was a wonderful sight to see the black Harley following Mum's coffin.

I had recovered myself by the time we got to the crematorium only to find streams of people waiting outside. I was completely overwhelmed. It took a great deal of self control to not just burst into floods of tears and the only way I could achieve that was to avoid interacting with anyone I didn't need to. I had to embrace close family, but everyone else would have to wait until after the service. We were all doing our best to hold it together. Mum's coffin was a very simple design and the flowers placed on top had been specially prepared by Mum's neighbour, Helen, who was a professional florist. The flowers looked wonderful, shades of purple, lilac and blue. Mum's favourite colours. All I could think was, mum would be impressed, and that was all that mattered to me.

The minister conducting the service was an amazing woman. She told us that she moved into her job from being a nurse. She had become fascinated by the way in which we (in the UK and the West) deal with death. She was very much of the opinion that it should be a celebration of life and yet so many of us struggle with letting go of our loved ones. We all agreed with her. She conducted the ceremony beautifully. The funeral bearers were the epitome of respect and professionalism. It was indeed a special ritual they were undertaking on our behalf and that really touched a place in my heart. I was so taken by the way they went about their duties that it gave me a new perspective on the ritual of saying goodbye. There were about 70 people who attended and every one of them that I spoke to after the ceremony said how wonderfully calm and peaceful it had been. They said they felt that the minister conducting the service knew Mum and that she would have been so proud of us all. That was all we could have asked for.

We went back to the golf club for the wake. This was a wonderful opportunity to celebrate Mum's life, with her closest and dearest friends, in the one place that had really been her passion (and second home) over her last 15 years. It was important to give Mum a final send-off, with a celebratory cheer, because that was one thing she had insisted on. She did not want people to grieve or feel sad, just to celebrate and have a drink 'on her'. We had arranged a spread of pictures of mum over the years, from her childhood, her wedding and various birthday and Christmas celebrations. Mum's closest friends were able to identify their parents in some of the pictures too. It was a wonderful way to connect people and also show the breadth of her life. She was more than a golfer, more than a mother and more than a worker. She was a very special person in the lives of many people. People ate and drank a toast and I read a final poem, 'Mum the golfer'. It was another end, and time to deal with the administration that follows all such events.

Spiritual-Logic Insights

Engaging with our Spiritual-Logic is to learn to give unconditional love in both our intentions and our actions – towards ourself and others. It is to appreciate the gift of life we have been given and to share that gift with others in support of the attainment of a higher level of human functioning. By higher level I am referring to our ability to function in ways that support others rather than impede others.

It is to have faith. Faith in ourself, our abilities, in others and in the fact that we are all connected at some level of our being – in a way that unites us rather than separates us. It is only our human logic fears that lead us to separate ourself from others. To have blind faith though is an error of human logic! Having faith in others is about knowing their boundaries and is always preferable to not trusting others.

We are designed to experience emotion – this is not a weakness, it is a part of the richness of our human experience and to deny ourself this is to create for ourself a life without depth and meaning. If we are emotional at the extremes, though, (excessive emotion or none at all) it is dysfunctional and our highest potential cannot be achieved because we are out of balance. We should not fear ours or another's emotions (whether we like the feeling of them or not). We should instead learn the messages they are sending so that we can navigate our life with a greater sense of purpose.

When we look at the breadth of another's life, from birth to death, we see with new eyes the gift that we had the honour to engage with in our own lifetime. To fail to recognise this before we, or they, die, though, has to be one of our greatest human 'sins', because in this lack of recognition we cannot fully appreciate the scope of what it means to be a human being. We cannot, therefore, fully appreciate ourself. The outcome of this is that we subject ourself to a life of pain and suffering, simply because we cannot see clearly.

Developing Spiritual-Logic

- ✓ Make choices in your life that you are prepared to be accountable for. You only have to answer to yourself. If you do not make a choice, then that is also your choice so don't blame anyone for it. Do not regret the choices you make, including the way in which you deal with death and dying.
- ✓ Be really clear about the positive impact the dying person has had on your life and you on theirs – it may have been a rocky road at times but you will have benefited greatly if you are willing to look – grown, learned, developed, experienced and lived. How you choose to interpret the experiences is your choice. Don't hold anything against another when they are alive or if they are dead.

- ✓ Another's death is an opportunity for new beginnings, should you choose to take advantage of them. This is not disrespectful – it is life. To not take advantage of your life is to truly disrespect those who could be living instead of you.
- ✓ Learn to work with your emotional responses in order that you can get the best out of yourself and others, to experience the richness that life offers without leading you into emotional dysfunction.
- ✓ Acknowledge that you have more control than you might wish to think and exercise that control with volition so that you may die peacefully, with gratitude and acceptance, should you get the opportunity to do so.

Another New Beginning

On one of the days I spent clearing out Mum's house I had to take Amelie over with me. She went bouncing into Mum's living room, looked at the empty bed that was now clear of all bedding, looked up at me, threw her arms in the air and said, 'gone!' My heart sank and sadness came flooding into me for a brief moment. Amelie then preceded to do all that she would have done if Mum had been there: fiddling with the ornaments; checking out this cupboard and that; just as if nothing had ever been any different. Such is the nature of a small child's way of engaging with life. She hadn't had sufficient exposure to her grandmother to feel any sense of attachment and therefore 'loss' was not a concept in her world. Of course she won't remember her grandmother, but her grandmother will continue to influence her life, that's for sure.

> *The purest example of what it means to be present is to 'see' through the eyes of a baby!*

Jakk gave birth to Mum's second grandchild, Matilda Primrose, on 30th October. Primrose was our grandmother, Gracie's middle name. Mum, was, and would have been so proud of Jakk. It was a home birth and all went smoothly. Tilly is a gorgeous little baby girl with a beautiful shaped head. Mum would have been so taken by little Tilly, who is a really cute and contented little baby. She would have in fact been ecstatic and a doting grandmother for sure. But life deals us all some cards and we have to work with them. No amount of us all wanting it, would have enabled Mum to be there for the birth given the cards she had been dealt. It just wasn't going to turn out that way and that is life.

S-L

There is a place for creating a vision of a future that you will not see – when we are children it is called dreaming. That ability doesn't go away because we are dying. To 'accept' does not mean we have to stop dreaming. To stop someone dreaming in order that they accept that they are dying is cruel and unnecessary. Our mind has the capacity for both – dreaming and acceptance. Mum being able to envision Tilly, before she died, gave her great comfort and peace.

As I sit now, just three months after the death of Mum and five days away from Christmas Day, things are, of course, very different than we had planned. We won't be going to Mum's this year. Mum is no longer suffering, and she did suffer. She hadn't wanted to die and I don't think she ever fully accepted the fact that she was. I hope I am wrong, because such a lack of acceptance of things we cannot control is probably the most painful of all our human experiences. I think the reality was that the tumour simply took her over and with it took her will, and that was that.

The year is drawing to a close and 2012 is coming around. It will of course be very different moving forwards. No one could have planned for the year just passed. Has it been a good or bad year? I cannot answer that question. I have watched a gorgeous four-month old grow and develop into a 16-month old, which has been an awesome experience. I have supported my Mum through one of the most difficult challenges of both of our lives. I have been surrounded and supported by an amazingly close family and my partner, and the incredible close friends of my Mum. As Mum would have said, 'it is all a learning curve'. Would I have wanted all the things to turn out as they did? No, most definitely not. But the world doesn't revolve around what I or anyone else wants, even though we might like to convince ourselves that it does. It revolves around something far more complex and we all have to work out how to handle it. I know that every person involved in managing Mum's condition over the year did the best that they could and I thank every single one of them for their contribution to caring for Mum, enabling her to maintain her independence for as long as was practically possible and enabling her to die with respect and dignity. She will live on through us all.

Mum came into this world as a function of two people connecting. If those two people had not met, Mum wouldn't have existed. If she and my father hadn't connected, I wouldn't have existed. If I had not gone on and lived the life I have, I would not have met my partner and our daughter wouldn't have come into this world either. But for a single decision, a look in another direction, a move, a thought, a change of mind... there are thousands of ways in which circumstances could have been different, just in terms of us actually getting here. Our arrival here is nothing short of a miracle. Once we are here, of course, there are millions and millions of decisions, choices, actions and influences that continue to guide us on our journey. Some of these things we will be aware of, many of them we are not aware of and may never see. Mum's influence will go on through all those she touched in her life.

Such is the nature of our eternity on earth. It is not in our physical presence here – that must end. It is in the fact that we entered into this life as a miracle and in the subsequent impact and influence we have had throughout our journey here – and that really is something to be truly celebrated rather than mourned. We have been given a gift in life – which is the honour to have been connected to all the other miracles here including those who die before we do. We must take the precious gift we have been given and do great things with it. In doing so, we evolve. Through our evolution, we also add value to the lives that have influenced us – making their life truly worth it!

A tribute to Mum is delivered in the poems I read at her cremation and the golf club, which I have included below, and is also in the telling of our story here. I am sure it is a story shared by so many. I hope that, one day, Mum's grandchildren will read our story so that they may know what a very special and unique person their grandmother was and fully appreciate the gift they have been given. May you find some relief in the sharing of our story and the Spiritual-Logic insights I have shared along the way, and may you find it in your heart to celebrate the life of those who leave before you. And, if you are fortunate to have the opportunity to share your dying process with others, that you are able to do so with acceptance, joy and peace along the way.

Spiritual-Logic Insights

Engaging with our Spiritual-Logic is to fully realise our highest potential and not to be constrained by the illusions of human logic that would result in us achieving less than we are capable of. It is to learn to 'see' that there is another world beyond the duality of our mind and our conditioned past, and to take the best of what we have been taught, to question for the purpose of understanding and to develop Wisdom.

Engaging with our Spiritual-Logic is to put fear into its rightful context rather than allow it to control and dominate our short and precious life. It is to learn the art of compassion, unconditional love, patience, acceptance, forgiveness and other such qualities that enable us to connect without attachment, give without wanting in return, and share without fear of recrimination. It is to respect and value all beings and appreciate the intricate and interconnected nature of our existence here together. It is to be in awe of the wonder of who we are.

It is to recognise that Spiritual-Logic is a part of who we are, and all that we can be. It is both our journey and the path to inner peace and contentment while living in this world, such that we may also be able to deal with the death of others with acceptance and joy. It is not so much a choice, but our evolution and our destiny, because it is of our Higher Self – our Spiritual Self.

Developing Spiritual-Logic

- ✓ Take the time to develop compassion for others and for yourself. Make it a priority in your life – give it the attention that it needs to achieve it.
- ✓ Really get to grips with the impermanent nature of all things and learn to feel a sense of comfort with that truth to enable you to 'let go'. Do not be fearful of this or feel out of control. It is about going with the flow of life – anything less is to swim against the tide. The tide will always win.
- ✓ Live life to the full, such that you can know every day, with every action you take, that you are living a life in which you will have contributed your very best… so you

can say your life was worth it. We may never know that we are close to dying, so live every day as if it were your last.

- ✓ Forgive at every opportunity you get, because to forgive others is to accept your own human fallibility.
- ✓ Learn to let go of your need for certainty, so you can fully appreciate what it feels like to go with the flow, with a sense of trust and faith!

You Are Not Gone

You are not gone, you are in me
You are in all that I see
Your presence is there in all that I do
You are in me and I in you.

The lessons you taught I will pass on
I see you in every one
In the sun and in the rain
You and me, we are the same.

In the thoughts I know we share
In the way we show we care
You are not here for me to see
You are there and now set free.

You are not gone you are in us
You would not want any fuss
So we smile and toast to you
And know you are in all that we do.

Mum The Golfer

Swing that club slow and true,
And just remember to follow through.
Down the fairway Mum's ball would fly,
Miss the bunker, she would cry.

Winning gave her such a thrill,
Losing was a bitter pill.
Always looking on the bright side,
Her keys to success, she did not hide.

Golfing made her life complete,
Beating her was no mean feat.
A demon with her putting stroke,
Put the fear of God in any bloke.

And now it's all a load of balls,
As she watches from the heavenly stalls.
She will live on in the trophies she's won,
And of course in her daughters and her son.

About the Author

Helen K Emms is a Thinker, Speaker, Mentor and Author, in Inspiring Spiritual-Logic. She helps people to achieve their highest potential by merging their spiritual intelligence with their human logic.

Helen Emms' charismatic and refreshingly honest approach together with her personal experiences within business, sports performance and life is shared with her clients through coaching/mentoring, workshops, speaking and her motivational books.

Helen balances compassion with thought-provoking challenge and an undeniable experience of the fact there is a more fulfilling way to live life than the way most people currently exist.

Helen's personal energy and passion for her work is infectious and has led others to want to undertake their life's journey through Inspiring Spiritual-Logic.

If you are interested in finding out more about how to develop yourself or others through Spiritual-Logic, you can visit Helen at www.helenkemms.com

Spiritual-Logic
You Are
Not Gone
Spiritual-Logic Reflections on
Loss and Bereavement
Helen K Emms
Inspiring Spiritual-Logic

"...a bible for all those who have suffered loss, an encyclopedia of how to live and how to die and a work of great beauty. It offers hope and consolation as well as understanding for all who struggle to find meaning in the mystery of life and death. Ultimately we are helped to find the peace, which passes all understanding."

Pam Hampton
Author of 'The Wisdom of the One Heart'

In this companion book to *Dying to Live: A Personal Journey Through Terminal Illness Using Spiritual-Logic*, Helen K Emms, shares 78 personal reflections and Spiritual-Logic insights to inspire you to feel more accepting, peaceful and joyful letting go of a loved one. Based on her experience supporting her mother through a terminal illness, Helen offers an alternative and uplifting perspective on death and bereavement including:

- Love and loss
- Celebration
- Human logic, Fear & Grieving
- Acceptance & Letting Go
- Compassion & Forgiveness
- Soul Contract & Connection
- Wisdom

60% of the Author's royalties will be donated to:
Brain Tumour Research, Iain Rennie & Brain Tumour UK.

ISBN: 978-1-906954-61-1 | **Format: Paperback**
Published: 20 September 2012 | **RRP: £14.99**

This book is a fitting tribute to a very special person in Helen Emms' life – her mum.

Helen has witnessed at first hand the devastation that the diagnosis of a brain tumour brings. She has used her years of helping people to achieve their higher potential through Spiritual-Logic to turn her own experience into something positive. She shares with you, the reader, some inspirational thoughts about how to deal with your own prognosis of a terminal illness or that of someone you love. We are honoured that Helen has chosen 'Brain Tumour Research' to benefit from sales of this book and hope it helps you in some way.

Sue Farrington Smith,
Director,
Brain Tumour Research

- 16,000 people a year are diagnosed with a brain tumour
- Brain tumours kill more children and people under 40 than any other cancer
- For brain cancer patients the five year survival is just 14% compared to 50% for all other cancers
- Yet brain tumour research receives less than 1% of the national spend on cancer

---

Despite following the advice of a wealth of best-selling self-help books, most of us still struggle to understand the fundamental laws and principles that govern the universe, our interactions within it and our ability to achieve success, health, wealth and happiness.

Have you ever wondered why the Law of Attraction doesn't work for you?

The answer is simple: The Universal Laws <u>*cannot*</u> *work in your favour until you identify and remove the psychological issues that are blocking your ability to live the life you want.*

In her ground breaking and easy-to-understand book, psychotherapist Deborah Sless, uses the concrete psychological theory of Transactional Analysis to uncover the secrets of the Universal Laws. **Beyond Our Illusions** takes you on a journey of self-discovery to understand:

- The Universal Laws and how they impact our lives
- Your own individual Life Story and the beliefs that were formed in childhood
- How to achieve freedom from your illusions and master your self
- The concept of Spirit as an energy force and how to tap into it

Genuine self-development is not easy but Deborah Sless provides her readers with the tools and framework they need - through clear explanations, examples and exercises - to begin a journey of self-discovery and change toward ultimate fulfilment.

ISBN: 978-1-906954-42-0 **Format: Paperback**
Publication: 1 August 2012 **RRP: £14.99**

DID YOU HEAR ME CRYING

The moving story of survival through 45 years of sexual, physical and emotional abuse

Cassie Moore

Lightning Source UK Ltd.
Milton Keynes UK
UKOW030121120912

198865UK00005B/16/P

9 781906 954574